Freedom
through frugality

[spend less, have more]

by Jane Dwinell

Spirit of Life Publishing
Montpelier, Vermont

Every effort has been made to ensure that website addresses referenced in the text are correct as of the printing date. Due to the fickle nature of the Internet, this information may change. Please act accordingly.

Published by
Spirit of Life Publishing
PO Box 243
Montpelier, Vermont 05601

Printed with vegetable-based inks on 100% recycled paper by
Queen City Printers, Burlington, Vermont

Edited by Marisa Keller

Cover and book design by Dana Dwinell-Yardley
Set in Adobe Jenson Pro and Helvetica Neue

ISBN 978-0-9799125-2-8

Printed in the United States of America

to Dana and Sayer,
who have taught me so much

Contents

Introduction

A time will come when you won't need this book because it will all be so obvious and second nature and just "the way we do things here." But that time has not arrived, so you do need this book. I need it, and I've been touting frugality for two decades. Frugality is a life art, and I'm still refining my ways of living it.

We need this book because we can't hear too often that frugality is freedom. By spending your money well and wisely, you can liberate the time you'd otherwise devote to earning more to buy more of what you don't really need.

Time is our most precious commodity. Like gold, it gains value precisely because it's limited. We'll spend a third of our lives sleeping and perhaps another third just doing life's daily tasks, like cooking, cleaning, schlepping, shopping, paperwork, and such.

When poet Mary Oliver asks, "What is it you plan to do with your one wild and precious life?" she is referring to those twenty-five remaining years of discretionary time. Some of those years, of course, will be devoted to making money to support yourself, but frugality can shave years off of your job life so that you can have a free life. Free for what? Ah, now that's where it gets so interesting.

Through frugality you can graduate from being a grousing laborer for someone else to being a master of your own fate. Who are you really? What do you love? What are you good at? What talents are unborn in you that want to live? What do you want to be your mark on the world? What is so important to you that you'd sacrifice for it? Frugality gives you the time to live who you are, not just as you must.

We need this book because we need to hear other people's stories of living well on less. If you only pick up ten good ideas here (and there are hundreds), you'll save money and feel so smart about doing it, you'll want to brag. Lord knows I can't help crowing, "Bought it for three dollars at the thrift store," when someone admires one of my long elegant dusters or my awesome cowboy boots. Reading Jane's ways of being frugal gives me good ideas that I can adopt or adapt, and confirms my good choices, makes me feel less like a stranger in a strange land. I used to say that my main task as coauthor of and spokesperson for *Your Money or Your Life* was to make the world safe for frugality. When I'd stand in front of groups or be interviewed for radio and TV, it was clear that I was healthy, well dressed, well fed (maybe too well fed), cheerful, intelligent, funny, and possessing all my faculties. It was as if to say, "Come on in, the water's fine."

Jane's stories are especially compelling because she has gone through several iterations of the frugal, free life. She has lived her dreams and has also shifted her strategies as her dreams have evolved. Frugality isn't just rural living with goats and chickens. It isn't just living in a wee space. It isn't just taking advantage of all the free fun available in cities. It's all of the above — and anything else — if that's what you want to do with your one wild and precious life.

We need this book because the world needs frugality right now. We are living beyond the means of the earth, spending more resources annually than can be restored, regenerated, or replaced. Experts agree that moderating the quantity and intensity of our resource consumption is a key to our survival. Some changes must come through smarter design, some through government policy. Many, though, will come through personal choice. Since Western societies are the biggest consumption culprits, and since we are steeped in the interpretation of freedom as being entitled to do whatever isn't expressly prohibited, the personal responsibility part of frugality is especially important. We need a solid rationale for choosing to moderate our consumption, because we'll be damned if we let someone else tell us what to do.

We also need this book because we need something to give to our friends, family, and coworkers when they think our choices will render us destitute and out of step with reality. This book is so interesting, readable, and kind (no rants or polemics to set your teeth on edge) that you can safely hand it to anyone whom you want to understand you or to follow in your footsteps.

I will treasure this book as I have treasured Jane's partnership over many years in bringing the *Your Money or Your Life* teaching to the world. Come on in, I say, the water of freedom — and frugality — is fine.

—*Vicki Robin*
Coauthor of Your Money or Your Life
www.yourmoneyoryourlife.info

Why be frugal?

1. How I became frugal

I wasn't always frugal: ask my parents and my friends. I have always loved books, clothes, and jewelry. As soon as I had my own spending money, I bought the complete works of Shakespeare (hardcover) and headed to the city to find the latest fashions. Once I had a job, I could be found scouting clothing, jewelry, and book stores for something to add to my collection. Never mind that I never found the time to read most of the books on my bookshelves (I still haven't gotten through all the Shakespeare) or that I was working as a registered nurse (RN) where high fashion and flashy jewelry were simply not worn.

It did begin to bother me that I was spending my days off shopping (or going to the movies, or eating out, or going on tropical vacations — other ways I found to pass my time). I finally began to realize that I was doing this because I was unhappy and didn't know what else to do. I liked my work well enough, but something was missing.

It wasn't always that way. I grew up the youngest of three children of parents who came of age in the Great Depression. My mother always sewed and knitted the family clothes, cooked from scratch, and told stories of how grateful my newly married parents had been for the fresh produce and meat that came from my grandmother's farm during the days of World War II rationing. My father always made sure there was a case of Campbell's tomato soup and Canada Dry ginger ale (both bought on sale) in the cellar for times of illness and need. They didn't have to do those things. My father had a good job, so my family was always comfortable and never lacked whatever we wanted. But my parents always claimed that frugality was inbred in both of them and that, even though they traveled extensively and had meat on the table every night, they could not help being careful with their money. Perhaps it was because they were careful how they spent their money that they could afford good steaks and roasts and around-the-world cruises.

Like many young people who came of age in the 1960s, I dreamed of living simply, as Henry David Thoreau and Helen and Scott Nearing espoused. I wanted to "go back to the land," have a self-sufficient homestead, grow my own food, and commune with nature. When I became an RN, I started saving money for that piece of land, bought books on gardening, house building, raising chickens, and growing grain, and purchased gardening tools and food preservation equipment. I lived frugally — carefully — with every action aimed toward the goal of my own homestead.

After a year of working at a big city hospital, I moved to the country with my books and tools. However, I discovered that homesteading was not all that it was cut out to be. There simply were too many things I, as a single person, could not do alone. It was a lot of work keeping up with the garden, chasing the wild animals away from the chickens and ducks, feeding the woodstove, and working full time. I gave up homesteading, feeling a complete failure, and turned to spending money instead.

Fortunately, as time went on, I met my husband, who also shared the homesteading dream (I hadn't really let it die). He also understood about frugality and the freedom that comes from spending money wisely, saving enough, and doing as much for yourself as you can. We looked at the amount of money we both had saved, and searched for a piece of land that was just what we wanted and was within our means. We bought that perfect piece of land, putting half the money down and taking a small, ten-year mortgage with the previous owners. We built a house and barn with the money we still had in the bank, raised animals and vegetables, and had a couple of children. Because both of us wanted to be home with our kids, we both chose to work part time off the homestead, and we managed to garner a small income from homestead products such as maple syrup and fresh produce as well. We had very little money and so much to do that we had to be frugal — with time and with money. Our life was rich, but it was also stressful. The hard work was good and satisfying, but we were isolated out in the country, raising two small children.

At that point I read a book called *Your Money or Your Life* (Vicki Robin and Joe Dominguez, Penguin Books, 1993; revised and reissued, Vicki Robin and Monique Tilford, 2008). This book helped to clarify for me that money, while necessary in our society, was simply one means to an end. The question was, What was the end I was looking for? What did I want out of life — the life that was not tied up with earning money, growing food, and raising children? How could I best go about getting it in a way that would work for my family and not cost us too much money? Being frugal made me happy; it was fun and it was challenging. But I wanted more freedom — the freedom that comes from having the right amount of money to do the things that I wanted to do.

This soul-searching led us to move across the country so that I could attend graduate school. We moved from the farm to a small city. We went from two parents each working part time and caring for children part time to one parent going to graduate school full time plus working part time, and the other parent staying home with the kids and running the household. We learned a lot from this two-year experience. We learned the value of each parent having time to pursue their own interests. We learned that we really did love living close to the land. But the big thing that we learned was that we didn't have to spend money to have fun in a city (unlike most of the people we knew), and that we could still have our values of simplicity and frugality wherever, or however, we chose to live. Not only did we come out of that experience not in debt (as most newly graduating students are) but also with enough money in the bank to buy a small pickup truck to drive back across country and to live on for the next year.

Time has moved on since then. When we realized that the farm work was going by the wayside because we were working off-homestead more and, in our nonwork hours, driving twenty minutes to a lake so we could sail and kayak, we sold our homestead and purchased a small cottage on the lake we loved (no mortgage involved). We winterized the cottage, began buying fresh produce and meat from our farmer friends instead of raising it ourselves, and boated to our hearts' content. We were still frugal — buying used boats and sports equipment, doing our own home repairs, heating with wood, preserving the produce we purchased, buying staple foods in bulk, and being careful with our vehicle and utility use — and since we spent more time at paid work, we began to have more money in the bank. We began to invest that money, hoping to someday have the freedom to not have to work for money at all.

After a few years on the lake, it was time to leave. Our wants and needs as a family were changing, so we moved to a very small city. We built yet another house, still debt free. We delved into these different surroundings where everyone had to make new friends and discover all the interesting things that came with living in town. We remained frugal, taking advantage of free events, a great library, a wider selection of farmers and their food, and better accessibility to walking, biking, and public transportation.

Eventually, in our mid fifties, we adults were able to retire from paid work because the income from our investments matched our needed living expenses. At the same time, our children came of age and moved off into their own (frugal) adult lives. With this next level of freedom, we were finally able to indulge our passion for travel and being on the water by buying a canal boat in France, where we would spend part of each year. We were grateful for all those years of creative, frugal living that allowed us to be comfortable living for an extended period of time on a boat with minimal amenities and less than 150 square feet of living space.

The story goes on. There will be more choices and changes ahead — of that we are sure. When the time comes, we know we will have the freedom to make whatever choices we want. We know we have the resources — financial and emotional — to face whatever is ahead for us. This incomparable freedom comes from nothing more than being frugal.

Frugal: careful, thoughtful, and with the awareness that our time is precious and that our choices do matter.

2. What is frugality?

What do you think of when you hear the word "frugal"? Do you picture little old ladies with drawers of old string, stacks of old newspapers, and more rags than any one person could ever use? Do you imagine eating rice and beans every night and never going out? Do you see old hippies living on a commune, monks in a cloister, or Okies making their way to California through the Dust Bowl?

Or do you see people who look like you, living comfortably — warm, dry, well-fed — and able to pursue the things that are most meaningful to them?

Here's how the Merriam-Webster dictionary defines frugal: characterized by or reflecting economy in the use of resources.

I'd have to agree.

Frugality is about being deliberate and careful with your resources

This includes the resources of time and money, the resources of your inborn and learned talents, the resources of your home and belongings, and the resources of your capacity to love and care for people, animals, and the environment around you.

Frugality is about respect

We are privileged to live in a wealthy society (even if you don't feel very wealthy). Chances are, if you're reading this book, you have a roof over your head, enough to eat, clothes on your back, and a minimum of comforts. While we in the First World may be tossed and turned by global and local economic developments, we are not apt to go hungry because our 100 acres of wheat was eaten by locusts or our potato crop was destroyed by disease, or become ill because our community lacks clean water and proper sewage disposal. We may have to cut back periodically on our small pleasures, but there's little chance of scurvy or starvation, cholera or malaria. However much money we have, we have more resources than most people on the planet. We should respect these gifts and learn to take care of what we have.

Frugality is about planning ahead

Because you understand your needs and desires, you can plan for them. You know you need some milk, so you pick it up on your way home from work so you won't have to go out again. You know you can get a better price, and the car you really want, if you start looking at the used car ads six months or so before you really need a replacement vehicle. You know you want to travel around the world sometime before you have children, so you avoid debt and start saving now. From the little things, like making sure you don't run out of shampoo or toilet paper, to the big things, like saving the money to buy a house, planning ahead is essential.

Frugality is about making do

It's about learning to make substitutions in recipes so you don't have to dash to the store for last-minute ingredients. It's about asking yourself if there's another way to get what you want or need than by going shopping and spending oodles of money. It's about caring for your things, repairing them, putting them away, and making them last. It's about wearing an outfit you already own instead of buying something new. It's about making popcorn for dinner when you're too tired to cook instead of taking everyone out for fast food.

Frugality is about understanding the true cost of things

That new cellphone that's such a deal is not necessarily such a deal. So, you throw out your old one — what are the landfill costs and the costs to the planet? What was the cost of manufacturing the new phone: the minerals that were mined by slave labor, the toxins left behind from the mining process, the factory and the factory workers that turn them out by the thousands, the oil used in transporting the goods to you? Beyond that, whatever monthly or per-call fee you're paying is more than what you would pay if you had no cellphone at all. It wasn't that long ago that people knew how to communicate without cellphones. What's the true cost of you being available to everyone all of the time?

Frugality is about not wasting anything — including your life

It means eating leftovers, using the milk before it spoils, and wearing the clothes that you already own or reading the books on your shelf you haven't read before buying more. It means talking through a conflict with a loved one before it gets ugly. It means quitting your job before your depression or your back pain gets any worse.

Frugality is about common sense

It makes sense to turn off the lights when you leave a room. It makes sense to walk or ride a bike instead of driving the car if your destination is less than a mile away. It makes sense to put your tools away instead of leaving them out in the rain to rust. It makes sense to buy the generic product that's half the price of the name brand. It makes sense to make dinner out of what's already in your fridge instead of buying more food. We were all born with common sense. Let's not forget to use it.

Frugality is about paying attention

It's about understanding your money, your home, your belongings, your health, your relationships, and your choice of activities. It's about understanding who you are, what gives you pleasure, and what doesn't. It's about spending your time and money in ways that are fulfilling to you.

That's what frugality is. Here's what it's not.

Frugality is not just about you

When you are being frugal you are being respectful of yourself and your personal choices while at the same time being respectful of your family and friends, the groups you belong to, the other people around you, and the planet you live on. Frugality is not selfish. On the contrary, frugality is about generosity and caring for everything and everyone.

Frugality is not about being cheap

It's not about stocking your house with stuff from the Dollar Store, always buying for the lowest price no matter what, or refusing to go out for beer and pizza with friends because then you'd have to spend some money. It's about knowing exactly what it is you want and need and finding a way to get that without spending too much money, not necessarily none at all.

Frugality is not about living a spartan existence

It's not about denying yourself anything other than the basics because it might cost you something, feeling you must wear every piece of clothing until you're in rags, using worn out or broken furniture just because it's there, or doing without fresh produce because you think it's too expensive. It's about living in basic comfort, however you personally define it, not how I define it or how society defines it.

Frugality is not about living in fear

Many of the Great Depression generation talk about this fear and can't seem to get away from it. Many people, of any age, hold onto the fear that they never know what's going to happen next, so they better not spend any money. They refuse to go out with their friends, take a trip with their spouse, or buy a replacement toaster when the one they've got shorts out every time they use it. Yes, it is prudent to be careful with our money, but if we have the cash set aside to cover six months' worth of living expenses and are not over our heads in debt, there's no reason to be afraid, financially.

We've all heard stories of an elderly person living in a shack somewhere, growing vegetables, raising a few chickens, not having a car, and rarely spending money, who ends up leaving a million-dollar legacy to some charity when they die. We don't know that person's motivation – they could have planned this on purpose or done it simply by accident. In either case, appearances can be deceiving – it's important that we don't make assumptions about the quality of someone's life solely by the appearance of their home, clothes, or car. The person who's drinking jug wine may have much more money than the person drinking Chateau Lafite. They may be happier, too.

What's your motivation for wanting to be frugal? Henry David Thoreau said, "I went to the woods because I wished to live deliberately, to front only the essential facts of life, and see if I could not learn what it had to teach, and not, when I came to die, discover that I had not lived." I'm not suggesting that we all live like Thoreau in a one-room cabin with a bed, a table, and two chairs (in case of a visitor). Far from it. But I am suggesting that by living frugally, you will be living as deliberately as Thoreau, and that you will have the freedom to really experience life to the fullest and not, when you come to die, discover that you have not lived.

There's no reason to be frugal just to be frugal. Frugality is simply a means to an end, an end where you can find peace and freedom. You can leave your financial worries behind and have more time to spend with loved ones and to pursue your passions. It's a wonderful way of life.

3. What's in it for you?

Frugal living is a wonderful way of life. I, and many other people who have chosen to live frugally, feel so many benefits that we cannot imagine living any other way. There is so much in it for you — things that are worth much more than the fleeting pleasure you may get from a Caribbean cruise that puts you in debt, from having a big house that impresses the neighbors but stresses you out, or from eating a high-calorie, high-cost meal out when you have plenty of food at home.

Here's what you will gain by living frugally.

You will have great security and no financial worries

What a relief! After years of being in debt and living paycheck to paycheck, you will have money in the bank and little or no debt. If you sell all the stuff you don't want or need, stop buying more unnecessary things, are more prudent about your utility use, cut back on watching TV and playing computer games, and discover low-cost/no-cost fun things to do, you will be able to save more money than you could imagine. You may get to a place where you go to work only because you want to, not because you have to.

With the unpredictable ups and downs of the global economy, and the stress of not knowing whether or not you will be the next person to lose their job, it pays off to have financial security. The national and global waves of economic instability won't affect you at all. While your friends and neighbors are living hand-to-mouth and are wondering whether or not they'll lose their house, you'll be living as you always do. You'll know that you (and your family) are provided for, so you will be able to relax and enjoy life.

If you learn to spend money with thought, not reflex, you will have money in your pocket at the end of the month. Eventually, you will be able to invest this money in prudent ways and have enough savings to help you and your family over any rough spots that do pop up.

You will have peace of mind and freedom

There is nothing like peace of mind. You will have few, if any, worries about money. You will fall asleep without anxiety and get up in the morning delighted to face the day, doing the things that you want to do, being with people that you love, and taking care of what has been entrusted to you. You will know that you are using your fair share and nothing more. You will be out of debt, have money put aside for a rainy day, and have the freedom to make meaningful choices. What more could you ask for?

Even if life throws you some curve balls and you face illness, tragedy, and sadness, it's a wonderful feeling not to have to worry about your money and your stuff in the midst of all of that extra stress. We all have problems at one time or another, but at least those problems won't be exacerbated by being in debt, facing clutter, paying high utility bills, or having nothing fun to do.

You will be able to make choices in your life. You will be able to respond to that inner voice that calls you to be an artist, to make quilts, to write books, to travel to the South Pole, or to bicycle across America. You will be able to have the time to give back to your community and to make the world a better place for those who need a helping hand. When your life comes to an end, whenever that may be, you will have lived a good life, a secure life, a free life, a caring life, and a fun life. That's a priceless feeling.

You will have better health

Chances are, once you start eating less junk food and more whole food, driving less and walking more, doing things that bring you happiness instead of anger, and spending less money instead of spending money you don't have, you will feel better physically. Some health improvements will come simply because you will have time to do the things you enjoy. Others will come from finally having the time to spend with your loved ones without having lingering fears about financial issues consuming your energy.

If you do have health problems when you start down this road, they may not disappear completely, but they may at least ease up. Many chronic conditions are exacerbated by air pollution, junk food, smoking, stress, and no exercise. Those conditions should improve, if not disappear. But even if you find some health problems lingering, you'll probably still have more energy and more excitement about your life. Your problems may seem to be less of a problem.

It's a pleasurable side effect that spending less money not only improves your health, it also improves the health of the planet. Doing things like walking or biking instead of driving, hanging up your laundry to dry, gardening, doing your own cooking, and not spending hours with your favorite electronic toy but playing catch with the kids instead will have a threefold benefit: you'll save money, get some exercise, and help the planet.

You will have more time for self, family, friends, and volunteering

If you're not out working more than forty hours a week trying to make ends meet or earning more money to buy more toys, you'll have more time for yourself and all the other people who mean a lot to you. If you're not staring at the TV every evening or spending hours commuting to a job you don't really like, you'll have more time to do fun, meaningful, and creative things. You will start to wake up happy every morning, eager to get on with the day.

Your family and friends will appreciate it, too. You'll have more time to spend with them talking, going for long walks, playing music, sharing a meal — whatever you like to do with other people. You'll even have time to make new friends, people who share your new interest in finding a different, more frugal way of life.

You'll also have time to volunteer for organizations that you support that could use your help. Whether that's your faith community, a social-issue group, or your local senior center, it doesn't matter. What matters is that you now have the time and energy to help others. Everyone involved benefits. Our nonprofit organizations could not do the good work they do without their volunteers.

You will feel good knowing that you are contributing to the solution, not the problem

You know our world is facing serious problems on many fronts. Issues like the lack of quality health care, ongoing war, bitter poverty, international terrorism, and the environmental consequences of climate change affect us all. Our world faces economic problems that are caused by many factors out of our control. The one factor we do have control over is the high personal debt load that contributes in its own way to global financial problems. Some people say that if we stop buying things, we're accelerating the downfall of the economy, but that's not the whole picture. By saving money in your local bank, by buying used goods from your neighbors, by supporting your local farmers, and by shopping at the locally owned stores in your downtown, you are helping the local economy in a big way — helping an economy that will help you if the global economy fails in an even bigger way.

Environmentally, you know that every time you choose to eat fresh food, purchase fewer paper products, use your electricity more prudently, and drive less, you are helping our planet. If we all chose to eat more locally grown food, we would guarantee that the landscape around us would stay green and cared-for. If we all consumed fewer paper products, we would save countless trees that are the lungs of our world. If we all reduced the amount of fossil fuels we use, at home and on the road, there would be less damage to the environment from oil drilling and oil spills, and we wouldn't need to build more power plants and oil refineries and engage in unnecessary wars. What could feel better?

You will be proud to be living your values

We all have values: those beliefs, standards, ideals, and principles that guide our lives. We want to live by them, but sometimes the push-and-pull of our busy lives keeps us from doing that. It's a great feeling to go through your day and, by your actions, know you are not compromising your particular values. Sometimes that's enough to get you through an uncomfortable time. Oftentimes, that heartache, headache, and hollow feeling in the pits of our stomachs come from not doing the right thing. Our parents and teachers taught us right from wrong when we were little, and it is up to us to follow through as adults.

Values are more than not committing crimes or stealing our neighbor's things, however. Personal values come from within and are not always dictated by society. You may have a value that says, "My partner comes first" or, "My career comes first." You may have a value of respecting and honoring animals that plays out as caring for strays, being careful not to use products tested on animals, and being vegetarian or vegan. You may have a value that says you will donate 10 percent of your income to charity. The list of personal values is endless. What are yours?

We may forget, or ignore, our values amidst all the activities of our busy lives. Sure, we want to drive less, but we forgot to go shopping on the way home, so we take another trip in the car. We may say we'll spend every evening with our children, but then something comes up at work and we stay overtime. When we're stressed and busy and not able to focus on what is important, we may leave our values (and our money) behind, which doesn't feel very good.

The internal gnawing can lead to stress-related health problems over time. It can lead to sleepless nights and a few too many beers and maybe some unintended rude behavior at work or at home. Having core values is an important part of being human. Actually living by those values is even more important. By using no more than your fair share of the world's resources, by using your money responsibly, and by spending time with your loved ones and yourself, you will be able to follow your values. It will feel great.

You will be building community

Whenever you make the commitment to drive less, shop at your small, downtown stores, and buy food from your local farmers, you are not just helping your local economy and environment, you are helping your community as a whole. We need strong downtowns to keep our communities vibrant and stable. We need to live in a place where people know each other and are committed to working together. We need to protect our local environment by keeping the farms in business, and not having them turn into another housing development or megamall.

Shopping and having fun closer to home means less driving, which means less air pollution, less need for more and bigger paved roads and parking lots, and more attention paid to pedestrians, bicyclists, and public transportation. All of this benefits your community. Supporting local businesses — from the stationery store to the bookstore, the women's clothing shop, and the pharmacy — means helping out your neighbors and keeping your city or town a bustling, lively place.

If you are also taking the time to get to know the people who live near you, bartering with friends and acquaintances, and inviting others to play croquet instead of computer games, you are helping to create community. If, and when, times get hard, we're all going to have to rely on our neighbors and friends: our community. If you don't already have it, building it is the next best thing.

You will be passing on an important legacy to the generations that follow

Being frugal is a choice for many of us, but for even more people — now and in the future — it will not be a choice. One of the best things we can do is to teach our children how to be frugal. If they learn while they're young how to cook, how to handle money, how to take care of their things, how to have fun without spending a lot of cash, and how to think twice before they ask for a new toy or game, they will be better prepared to be adults who are not in debt or stressed about money.

They will also be in a better place to deal with whatever changes lie ahead for the world's population, economy, and environment. The day may come when driving a car, eating out-of-season foods, or turning on the lights will be a luxury only the wealthiest can afford. Children who learn to be frugal when they're young will be able to weather these possible changes in a better way.

At one workshop I led for a group of ten- to twelve-year-olds about these issues, we talked about how petroleum products were in almost everything we consumed, in one way or another — from manufacturing to transportation to farming to electricity. We discussed ice cream cones, for example: how each aspect of that final product was touched by fossil fuels and how their mint chocolate chip treat cost more than the price they paid for it. As the world's energy needs grow while the world's oil reserves shrink, these kids knew they would most likely live in a different world as adults.

One girl, not content with all this, said to me, "Why do you grown-ups keep telling us we have to fix the problem? You created it — you should fix it." She's right, of course. What kind of world are we leaving to our young people? The time to start changing how we spend our money and use our resources is right now.

4. You will be challenged

Until being frugal is a well-ingrained habit, you will face challenges. It won't always be easy to do things differently from what you're used to and from how most people around you are doing things. Although many people talk about "cutting down" in tough times and living within their means, it's human nature to start spending again once the money returns. Becoming frugal as a way of life means that you won't change when the economy changes.

The task of learning to be frugal is a big job and an ongoing process. It will change the way you look at everything you do, the decisions you make, and how you spend your time and with whom. It will challenge your assumptions about what society — parents, teachers, the media, and other people and organizations — has taught you and continues to teach you. For a while, it will feel as though you are swimming upstream.

I've led workshops on this subject over the years, so I can already hear your litany of "what ifs?" You may be concerned about what friends, family, and coworkers will think of you. You may be concerned that your children will be ostracized in school, made fun of, or teased. You may worry that you'll disappoint people, that your spouse will leave you, or that you never will get out of debt. You may fear that you will not "get ahead." You may be afraid of being different or of challenging the prevailing "wisdom."

After all, you are expected to follow the rules in our society, and, by making different choices about how you spend your time and money, by not buying into the latest fad in electronics, by choosing to work part time or not at all, you will no longer be following the rules. You may be asking, "But don't I need to have a mortgage to get the tax deduction?" That loses importance if your income is lower. "But don't my kids need to go to college?" Not necessarily: it all depends on what they want to learn and what they envision their lives to be like as adults.

You may want to gather like-minded souls around you as you practice frugality, because it will be hard, and at times you will want to stop. You can find others through simplicity study circles held at churches or community centers. There are online study and support groups. If you have frugal friends, ask them to mentor you. Or you can just get started, talk about it with your friends and neighbors, and see who might want to join you. There are many possibilities.

In the meantime, here are answers to some of the concerns and challenges you may have as you head down this path.

My family doesn't want to do this

Not everyone wants to think about their money, their belongings, where they live, how they get around, and what they do. If you're interested, but your partner isn't, you may have to go it alone at first. Eventually, he or she may see the positive results from what you're doing and want to participate. At some point, you may want to make some bigger changes like moving to a smaller house, a new community, or a different part of the world altogether. You may even want to leave the relationship you're in. It's hard to predict what may happen as you become frugal; you're building another kind of self-awareness.

Don't push your partner (and older kids, if you have them) if they don't want to do this. Try out some changes and see where they lead. When you go through the house to catalog all that you own (Chapter Nine: Stuff), go ahead and catalog everyone else's belongings — with their permission, of course. Only sort those items that are yours alone and things that everyone else agrees you can sort. As you learn things about yourself and your life, share them.

When you're ready to start making some changes, make them within the area of the household you are responsible for. If you're the usual cook or grocery shopper, then begin to follow the food suggestions in chapter seven. If you're responsible for cleaning the house or doing the laundry, follow the suggestions for frugal housecleaning and ways to do laundry (Chapter Six: Home). If you have your own car, choose to take public transportation, bike, or walk to work instead of driving (Chapter Eight: Transportation).

If you're in a long-term relationship, find out why your partner doesn't want to participate. If it's simply that they don't like dealing with things like this, but have no quibble with your redesigning the household, then go for it. If your partner really likes the big house, the latest toys, and his or her high-powered career, spend some time thinking if such a clash of values can work in your relationship. Find subtle, and not so subtle, ways to engage the people you live with.

It is possible to do it alone even if you live with other people. Don't let that stop you.

I don't have the time to do things for myself

Living frugally takes more time, in some ways. When you cook from scratch you have to remember to soak the beans or make the bread. When you hang your clothes up to dry, you have to plan ahead. When you have a garden, you have to wait for the tomatoes to ripen. You may be used to paying people to clean your house, cook your food, dry clean your clothes, mow your lawn, and plow your driveway. You may be used to carrying a cellphone with you all the time and used to being instantly connected with the rest of the world.

As you look at your finances, you may realize that you don't want to be paying all these people to do all these things for you. You may realize that you would rather work part time and earn less money but make up for it by taking care of household chores yourself. You may realize that being at the beck and call of everyone is just stressing you out. These are things to consider, and make choices about, on the way to freedom through frugality.

Being able to pay for services and special gadgets is a privilege of living in our society. But the merry-go-round of working more to earn more to pay for the things we feel we need gives us less time to take care of ourselves, and so we pay, and then we need to earn more. It's a vicious cycle. You may find that you prefer to get off the merry-go-round and do things for yourself. You will learn how to plan ahead as you experiment with cooking from scratch, finding another way to get places than by hopping in the car, handling your own household maintenance, and entertaining yourself.

Don't try to do everything at once. Choose one thing to do in one area, and add others as you feel comfortable. Use small successes to keep you motivated to try new things.

I'm afraid I'll miss out on the latest _____

You may miss out on the latest, but what does that mean to you? Are you afraid you'll miss fun conversations with your coworkers if you haven't watched the big TV hit or learned about the newest computer? Are you concerned that people will think less of you? Do you think that if you miss out on the latest, you will miss out on a special, or life-changing, experience?

We fill our lives up with so much clutter — of different kinds and for different reasons. Feeling that you have to keep up with the latest whatever is just another form of clutter. There are so many things to do in life: compelling, interesting, and important things that have nothing to do with television, electronics, shopping, or gadgets. Taking the time to consider how you want to spend your money allows you to figure out what really is compelling, interesting, and important to you. Most people discover that being with family and friends, spending time in nature, reading a good book, and/or doing something creative are the most meaningful things they can do.

I stopped watching television in 1984. Sure, I have a hard time with some clues in crossword puzzles, and other references to popular programming out there in the world, but I don't miss those hours I spent in front of the idiot box. I don't read a daily newspaper anymore, either, and don't miss it in the least. I have found so many more fun things to do with my time, and I know I have yet to discover them all. You can make conversation with your coworkers and friends about all the new things you discover when you stop worrying about what you might be missing.

Get rid of my excess stuff? But what if I don't have enough money to get more?

Most of us are attached to our stuff for one reason or another. Our stuff has emotional ties, sentimental ties, status ties, and financial ties. We accumulate stuff for all these reasons: someone gave it to us, we bought it for an important event, we paid a lot of money for it, we've been lugging it around for years, it gave us happy times.

We fear getting rid of our (unused) stuff: What if I can't afford more? Will I go homeless, clothing-less, and hungry, and be without my toys and entertainment? What would I do without a car, a boat, a computer, a TV, my power tools, my food processor, and every letter I received from my mother?

Our stuff will not protect us from tragedy. Our stuff will not make us important, or athletic, or interesting. Our stuff is just our stuff. The emotions attached to our things lie in our heads, not in each pair of pants, each plate, each chair, or each pair of earrings. Our memories lie within us as well. We will still have them even if our stuff is gone — ask people who have suffered a calamity like fire, flood, hurricane, divorce, or death.

I expect that, barring the most tragic situation, you will always have enough stuff, enough to eat, and a roof over your head. In any case, holding onto all your stuff won't keep you from homelessness or hunger. Although getting rid of the stuff you don't use or love may feel bad or scary, it won't destroy your life. As you go through your things and get in touch with what's really important, you will have a better sense of what to keep, what to let go of, and what you might want in the future. And the extra cash and extra space will certainly come in handy.

I'm not suggesting that you get rid of all those things that do hold memories, like love letters, your grandmother's engagement ring, photos of your children, or a mug your best friend brought you from Europe. Keep these things, use them, and cherish them. What I am suggesting is that beneath the memories and the fears, the wishes and the hopes, is a whole lot of stuff you never use that someone else could. We need to learn to share.

How will I know I've succeeded if I don't have an important career, a big house, and lots of stuff?

So much of our ego and our sense of ourselves is tied up in the things we own, the job we hold, and the way we spend our leisure time. I meet people over and over who fear being looked down upon by family and friends if their house is not as big and as well-equipped as other people in their "class"; if they don't have a well-paid, full-time job (landed with a college education); and if they don't take expensive vacations to the latest popular spot. Even people who do not have much money look to those "above" them and go into debt to buy a widescreen TV, to attend community college (when they hate school and would rather work in one of the trades), or to spend a week at the beach when they can barely put food on the table.

We all want to feel good about our lives and be accepted by others. But whatever happened to qualities like generosity, compassion, thoughtfulness, integrity, honesty, creativity, and wisdom? Is any one of these qualities not better than a 4,000-square-foot house, a week on a Caribbean island, a speedboat, the latest electronic gizmo, a Ph.D., or a brand-new car?

If we stop striving for bigger, better, more, and more, we will be different than many people we come into contact with. But do they really care? Won't they be more impressed with you if you listen to them, offer to help them, and not expect anything in return?

Society (primarily the schools, the media, and the advertising industry) gives us the "values" that so many strive for today. But it is OK to do things differently. In some circles, people will think better of you for living in a smaller house with less stuff, working part time, and doing what moves you. What matters the most, though, is what you and your immediate family think of yourselves. When people get seriously ill or disabled, have a natural disaster or accident befall them, or come close to death, they no longer worry about what anyone else might think of them. Their most intimate loved ones are the most important, and it doesn't matter what kind of house they live in, what kind of clothes they wear, or what car they drive. We want close, meaningful relationships. You don't need any stuff or a high-powered career to have those.

I don't like being different from others — and won't my kids get teased?

Parents supply their children with the latest in fashion, technology, sports equipment, and toys mainly so the kids won't feel left out among their peers — and sometimes with good reason. Kids can be notoriously mean to other kids. At the same time, the same parents, after supplying their kids with the latest everything, are sure to supply themselves as well. After all, who wants to feel left out at work or be different from their friends?

Not all people — young or old — look down on their classmates, coworkers, or friends because of what they do or do not have. Friends are friends, whether they're sliding down a snowy hill on a piece of cardboard or on the latest high-tech sled. Friends are friends, whether they are sharing a bottle of inexpensive wine sitting together on the front porch, or sipping a more expensive bottle at the local bistro. Friends want to spend time together, and they don't need the latest toy or the fanciest restaurant to do that.

I imagine that when you remember your childhood, you probably remember times with your friends splashing around in a lake or a pool in summer, building a fort in the woods, playing hopscotch marked on the sidewalk with chalk, or riding your bikes around the block. When you see pictures of children in Third World countries, they're happily playing soccer with a makeshift ball or tending to their homemade dolls. All the world's children, by nature, are creative and inquisitive and know how to make their own fun — if we adults will only get out of their way.

We adults, too, can take a hint from those memories and plan to spend time with friends and loved ones at a local park, sitting around the fire talking on a snowy evening, playing a few hands of cards, going for a bike ride, or hiking a nearby mountain. There are wonderful, creative, and interesting ways to spend time together without spending a lot of money. If your friends would rather meet you at the mall, you may want to rethink your friendship.

It's human nature for some people to tease or look down on others for being different; it's a way for them to feel better about themselves by feeling superior to others. It doesn't feel very good, whatever your age. Be prepared for a few hurt feelings for every member of the family as you move down the frugality road. Don't be surprised if you lose a few friends, but expect to gain some new ones, too.

I want to eat what I want, when I want, and where I want!

We are spoiled by the vast array of food that is available to us twenty-four hours a day. Any desire can be fulfilled at a whim. Chips and dip, bagels and cream cheese, strawberries, steak, chicken fingers, chocolate, and oranges are available nearly everywhere, any time. We can stop at a mini-mart, a burger place, a pizza place, a fried-chicken joint, a hot-dog stand, a Mexican eatery, or a Chinese restaurant almost anywhere we happen to be. With refrigeration, air transport, and more eating and grocery shopping places than are really necessary, we have the world's foods at our fingertips, and we're used to it. We're used to having sliced tomatoes and cucumbers on our salads all year 'round. We're used to having a wide array of fresh fruit all the time. We're used to going out to eat whenever we feel like it. We're used to having New Zealand lamb, Swiss chocolate, Dutch cheese, and Chilean wine. Gone are the days when food choices were limited, when dinner tended to be meatloaf, mashed potatoes, and canned green beans, and when your family went out for a meal once a year on Mother's Day.

Eating anything you want when you want it can be an expensive proposition. If you eat foods out of season — apples in July, strawberries in January, and peaches and plums in April, for example — they won't taste very good and will be much more costly. If you drop into a convenience store or a take out place because your forgot to bring some snack foods with you in the car, you'll pay for it in the long run. If you eat at restaurants day in and day out, not only will you spend extraordinary amounts of money, but dining out will eventually seem less fun.

It's important to take pleasure — and gain nutrition — from the food we eat. By being thoughtful about your food choices, eating in season, going out to a restaurant only for special occasions, and choosing whole foods over junk foods, you'll save money and eat better at the same time. Don't forget to indulge your passions for certain special foods now and then — New Zealand lamb, Swiss chocolate, Dutch cheese, and Chilean wine certainly are delicious, in moderation.

I don't want to have a boring, drab life

Many people equate frugality with hard times, chapped hands from hanging laundry out in the cold, a family huddled in the kitchen trying to stay warm and eating nothing more than peanut-butter sandwiches, and children going without health care and dying of something treatable like an ear infection or a puncture wound.

That's not the kind of frugality I'm talking about. Yes, there are many people in our country and in our world who do live in dire poverty and who don't have a choice about how they wash and dry their clothes, what they eat, and whether or not they get health care. They are simply getting by the best they know how.

I'm talking about paying attention to how you spend your money — and your time — so you won't have a boring, drab life. When you know what you really want out of life, you may be happy to hang clothes on the line, and make do with secondhand furniture, peanut-butter sandwiches, and less health care so you can pursue your dreams. Whether your dream is to sail around the world, climb the tallest mountains on each continent, write the great American novel, play your musical instrument with more pleasure and skill, take in foster children, go to law school, nurture AIDS orphans in Africa, or be an active participant in your municipal government, you will be able to follow through using the time and money you will gain by being frugal. That sounds anything but drab and boring.

I hate change — it's so hard and takes so much time

The old saying goes that nobody likes change except a wet baby, and I've known a few wet babies who didn't like to be changed, either. Change is hard. Know that and accept that and find ways to help you deal with the challenges.

There seem to be two schools of thought about how to create lasting change in your life, two very different ways.

One school of thought is to do things gradually, slowly, and deliberately, in small steps. First you educate yourself, next you try some simple steps and, with success, you take bigger and bolder steps. The change you wish to create will come in time if you stick with it. It's just like the old wisdom that if you do something new like floss, exercise, or eat differently, it takes three weeks before it becomes a habit and you'll feel funny if you stop.

The other school of thought is that lasting change only comes through extreme, abrupt, and radical change. No simple steps, you just go for it: move to smaller house; start taking public transportation; and ditch the TV, the food processor, the fast food, and the designer coffee.

Either way, it's not easy, and there will be setbacks and stresses. Only you know yourself and what will work best for you. The choice is yours. The important thing is to start becoming frugal: take the time to consider the difference between your needs and your not-so-necessary desires, and how much money you really need to have the life you want. It may be best to change everything all at once. It may be best to make one change every day, every week, or every month. Some things are easier and take little time and effort. Others are harder and more complicated.

It takes time to change old habits and create new ones. Find the way that will work best for you.

Remember, this isn't "simple living." Living life mind-fully and respectfully and taking the time to do things for yourself can be a very complicated thing. There are so many choices to make and questions to ask and things to consider. You may get tired of it all and just want to go out for pizza and beer. So do it. This is not about living in constant struggle or having a martyrdom experience. This is about looking deeper and living more fully. Sometimes that's simply about having pizza and beer and hanging out with your good buddies.

5. You do have a choice!

One of the most common choices we have as individuals is how to spend our money. No one is standing over us at the grocery store telling us we must buy the carrots instead of the zucchini. No one is following us around as we look for a place to live, saying we must choose a condo and not an apartment. No one forces us into a Honda when we really want a Toyota. We get to choose.

It may feel like we can't really choose, however, and that society, and all the authority figures in it, is telling us what to do. We may feel like we'd disappoint our spouse or our friends if we made different choices than they would. We may feel like we're being irresponsible if we don't have life insurance, health insurance, and homeowner's insurance. We may feel like we're not being good parents if we don't buy Legos for our children, take them to Disneyland,

and send them to college. We may feel embarrassed if we don't fit in with our neighbors.

I'm not suggesting that you buck the system just to buck the system, or move your family to fifty acres in the wilderness and start living off the land (not unless that's what you all want to do). I am saying that you do have choices about many aspects of your life and how you spend your money, whatever your current financial, employment, and personal situation.

For example, everyone needs a home, but you don't have to own one, or own one in the "right" neighborhood.

Everyone needs to eat, but you don't have to have a kitchen complete with microwave, popcorn popper, bread machine, toaster oven, ice-cream maker, blender, pasta machine, food processor, juicer, mixer, electric knife sharpener, espresso machine, thirty-cubic-foot stainless-steel refrigerator, and a double-oven, six-burner-with-griddle range.

Everyone needs to quench their thirst, but you don't have to do it with fancy mineral water, sports beverages, energy drinks, tall lattes, fresh-brewed chai, Koolaid, or sixty-four-ounce soft drinks.

Everyone needs to get around, but you don't need a new car — of any price — to get you where you want to go.

Everyone needs a bed to sleep in and a place to bathe, but to sleep well and stay clean you don't need designer linens and towels, high-end body-care products, a bed large enough for a family of five, and a shower with multiple heads.

Everyone needs to take care of their bodies, but you don't need multiple doctor visits for a litany of minor complaints, health insurance that covers every possible scenario, a plethora of pharmaceuticals (legal and illegal), and a hairstyle that costs more per year to maintain than the Gross National Product of Mali.

Everyone wants to have fun and to use their minds and bodies in new and creative ways, but you don't have to get a widescreen TV with hundreds of channels, a DVD player, a stereo with floor-to-ceiling speakers, a digital camera, a computer, a Wii, an iPod, a cellphone, access to the Internet, and every piece of sports equipment imaginable.

Everyone wants the best for their children, but that doesn't have to include fancy strollers, cases of disposable diapers, regular trips to the amusement park, a roomful of plastic and electronic toys, brand-new clothes, and an Ivy League college education.

Everyone needs an income to pay for those things that only money can buy, but you don't have to work full time, have a long, expensive commute, be stressed at the end of the day, or stick with a job you hate just because the "benefits" are good.

You do have a choice — in these and in other aspects of your life. There are many different ways to get what you need and want in life. You don't have to do things the way everyone else does, or the way you assume everyone else does. Your only limit is your imagination, not your wallet.

We are all different, with different passions and desires, favorite activities, and not-so-favorite activities. It is up to us, as individuals and as families, to figure out what we want out of life.

One way to discover that is to ask ourselves each time we start to spend money on something — whether it's a house, a car, a plane ticket, or an apple — Is this what I really want? Does it make sense to spend this much money on this thing? How many hours did I have to work (or will have yet to work) to earn the money to buy this thing? Why do I want this thing? Is there another way to get what I want without spending this much money?

If you think before you act, understand your motivation for wanting to acquire this thing at this time, and make a choice that fits your values, fits the vision of your life, and fits your finances, then you are frugal.

It's that easy, and that challenging.

We are overwhelmed with choices in our society. Even if we stop watching commercials and stop reading the newspaper, it's hard to get away from the twenty-four-hour convenience stores, the mega-malls, and the big box stores. We can buy anything new that we might want, at almost any time of the day, and probably within an easy drive of just about everywhere but the deepest wilderness and widest prairie. And if we're out in that prairie or that wilderness, or even if we're in the middle of a big city, we only need to go on the Internet or turn on a shopping channel to spend money. No wonder it seems next to impossible to be frugal.

But it is possible to be frugal. By being conscious and respectful, creative and deliberate, and by making do and planning ahead, this wonderful thing called frugality will give you the time and opportunity to do those things that are important to you. By making the choice not to get wrapped up in the consumer mentality that bigger and newer is always better and that you must keep up with your neighbors, you can slow down and appreciate what you do have. By taking a chance and being open to possibilities, you will find a whole new world waiting to be explored.

That sounds like freedom to me.

The next nine chapters will give you some ideas about how to bring frugality into your life. You may think that many of these ideas are silly and can't possibly save you much money, but put together they will add up to plenty. Saving $10 a day will net you $3,650 in a year, $20 a day will get you $7,300. Add to that the beauty of compound interest, and, in no time, you'll have a serious amount of cash to help you live your dreams.

So, try out these ideas one at a time, one category at a time, or pick and choose your favorites. Once you start implementing small changes, the rest will start to flow, and your bank account will grow. Before you know it, frugality will be a wonderful new habit, and you'll find it hard to turn back to your old way of life. Good luck!

How to be frugal

6. Home

Most of us in the First World are fortunate enough to have a roof over our heads, clean running water, reliable electricity for lighting and appliances, and access to enough fuel to keep us warm in cold weather and cool in hot weather. In fact, our homes use more of our financial resources than any other aspect of our lives. Whatever kind of place we live in — whether rented or owned, a house, an apartment, a condo, a camper, a boat, a yurt, or a log cabin — we need money to pay for it, care for it, heat and cool it, furnish it, clean it, insure it, and find time to enjoy it.

There are many ways to cut the cost of paying for all the aspects of the place where we live and to reduce the time it takes to maintain it.

The following are some ideas to help you have a frugal home.

Consider where you live

Why do you have a place to live? What do you do there? What do you like to do there? What do you want to do there?

If your home is primarily used for sleeping and storage space, you clearly don't need a very large or fancy home. On the other hand, if you work at home, care for an elderly or disabled family member, homeschool your kids, have a hobby that takes up extra room, or love to entertain, the space will mean something different to you.

Do you feel crowded in a small place? Do you love tall ceilings and large windows? Or do you prefer dark walls and a more cave-like feeling? Do you have an avocation that requires a certain amount of space, or a certain amount of quiet and privacy? Do you and your family like to gather in the evenings and play cards or board games, or sit around the television?

Do you have a yard of any kind? Is it too big or too small? Do you have outbuildings — a shed, garage, workshop, or playhouse? Do you like the location of your home? Can you walk or bike to work or school, to shops, library, church, or synagogue? Or do you need to drive some distance to services?

Are you living in the right home? As you consider where you live and where you might like to live, think about how you might use your current space differently and more in tune with your needs. You may have too much space that is rarely used, or not enough space.

If you have a guest room for your sister when she comes every summer for a week, and it is never used at any other time, you could consider paying for her to stay in a local motel or bed-and-breakfast instead of heating, cleaning, insuring, mortgaging, and furnishing a rarely used guest room. She actually might appreciate the privacy. And if you're used to having at least one night together for settling down in your nightclothes for a long, deep heart-to-heart, you can always plan on spending that one night with her in the motel!

The same goes for that formal dining room you use a few times a year to entertain friends. Consider having a backyard barbeque, a party at a local park, a simple meal of finger foods and beverages served in the living room, or splurge on a restaurant meal for everyone. It may be cheaper than paying for that little-used formal dining room.

If, on the other hand, you feel your house is too small for your needs, the kids are in your hair all the time, and you never have any peace and quiet, think about how you could rearrange your space. Maybe the play area could be next to the kitchen instead of next to your bedroom where you're trying to read or write. Maybe you can install room dividers or bookcases to give a sense of privacy. Perhaps you could paint the walls a lighter color, knock down a wall, raise the ceilings, or add a window on the south side. Perhaps you are in a climate that would allow you to use your outdoor space more often.

Where we live is important. It expresses who we are as well as giving us shelter and protection from the elements, and it provides a space for day-to-day living. There are many ways to create a home. Before you can create the home you really want, in a way that makes sense for you financially, you have to know what's important for you and the people you live with.

Know what your home costs you

Eventually, you will be tracking all of your expenses (Chapter 13: Money), but, for now, find out what your home costs you. Calculate mortgage payments (divided into principal and interest) or rent, utility costs (heating oil, firewood, electricity, propane or natural gas, water and sewer, trash and recycling, telephone — land line and cell — Internet service, cable), property taxes, insurance, upkeep and maintenance. Don't forget to include cleaning supplies, gas for the lawnmower, condo fees, flowers for the garden, and the average amount you spend yearly on new appliances or decorating. If you hire out lawn mowing, snow removal, house cleaning, and maintenance work, include these costs as well.

Financial advisors recommend that you spend no more than 30 percent of your income on the cost of your home. Once you know what your home costs you (and what your total income is), you can determine your percentage. If it's more than 30 percent, you'll need to take some serious cost-cutting measures. As you follow the money-saving ideas that follow, keep track of your expenses and see how much you can reduce them. You don't have any control over your rent or your property taxes (unless you move), but everyone can lower their utility bills and the cost of maintenance and upkeep.

Determine the square footage of your home

This is easy. You may already know your square footage. If you don't, simply measure the length and the width of your home and multiply those numbers. Don't forget to double the figure for a two-story home, or triple for three stories. If your home is not a square or a rectangle, you will need to measure each part, multiply the length by the width of each, and add all these figures together.

A 20-by-30-foot one-story home is 600 square feet; if the same building is two stories, it's 1,200 square feet. If you include the 10-by-16 wing that contains the den, you'll have another 160 square feet to add to the total.

If you are in an apartment, condo, or other type of home, the same rules apply. Measure your living space, multiply the length by the width, taking into account multiple stories and odd shapes, and you'll have your square footage.

Now that you know the square footage, consider this: people can live quite comfortably and economically in a home that is no more than 300 to 400 square feet per person. Doesn't that sound better than living in a home that's really too big for your needs, and expensive to heat, cool, clean and insure? How does your current home add up?

Move to a smaller home

Unless you already live in a home that is 300 to 400 square feet (or less) per person, it's time to consider moving — or sharing. You may not be able to do this right away, or even think you can, but it is worth looking into. Smaller homes are generally less expensive to purchase or build, and there is less to maintain, heat and cool, insure, and clean. You may be able to sell your current home and buy a smaller, less expensive home with the money from the sale — and even manage to ditch your mortgage at the same time.

You may want to take this opportunity to consider whether you want to rent or own, whether you want to live in a single-family house, a condo, a duplex, or an apartment. Consider the children in your life — what age they are, if they live with you, if they've left home, or if you don't want to have them (or not yet). Children are remarkably flexible about their living space. Siblings may be happy to share rooms. Grown children no longer need their own rooms; when they come to visit, they can sleep on a pullout couch or at a nearby campground or inexpensive motel. If you have, or will have, a baby, remember that infants and toddlers don't even need their own room.

Think of this as an opportunity to move closer to your work or to a neighborhood, town, or part of the country you prefer. Look for a home has the amenities you are looking for, whether that is garden space, room for your hobby or home business, or a place to store your camping equipment, your skis, or your bicycles. Look for a home that is energy efficient or can be remodeled to become so. Look for plenty of natural light and insulation and a floor plan that makes sense or can be easily modified, as well as the usual considerations such as a good foundation and roof.

Take your time with this decision: it's one of the biggest decisions you'll make, and certainly the most expensive. Build a new home, if you prefer, and take advantage of the advances in energy-efficient building techniques. Or find a place that already exists that you would be happy to call home for a long time, and renovate it to suit your needs.

If you build or renovate, look for good-quality used building materials, fixtures, lighting, and appliances. There are many houses that are being torn down that have perfectly good things in them that can be reused. Look for used-building-equipment supply places, or check the ads online or in your local paper.

Perhaps you would prefer to rent rather than own. You won't have a mortgage to deal with, or maintenance problems. It's easier to pick up and move if you want to. If you have a cooperative landlord, you'll be able to make cosmetic changes such as new paint or wallpaper. Check to make sure the rental unit is weatherized, so that you aren't paying too much in utility bills. Look for other things you may want, such as garden space or a safe, outdoor play space for the kids to use. You can also look into housesitting—if you are up to moving frequently—or renting a home very inexpensively that you can only use for part of the year. There are many more housing options than owning your own place. As much as home ownership is touted as a good investment and a way to feel you have succeeded, it's also a lot of work, and may cost you more than renting.

If, for whatever reason, you are unable or unwilling to move and you have a home that exceeds the recommended size, consider sharing your home with others. We are unfamiliar with this in our culture, and it may be an uncomfortable thought. Many folks, however, are finding that sharing living space broadens their horizons, increases their sense of community, and brings in some extra money.

Consider renting a spare room to a college student, a single person, or an elderly person. You could house an exchange student or take in foster children. You could offer your extra space to a friend who needs a quiet place to write, paint, or compose music. You could sign up with an international travel group where people offer a place in their homes to people on the road — it's a wonderful opportunity for both you and the traveler. Perhaps a non-profit organization you work with needs storage space or a small office. There are many possibilities. Think about what might work best for you, your home, and your life.

Weatherize your home

You will use less energy to heat and cool your home if it is properly insulated and all the cracks and crevices are closed up. You can hire someone to do an energy audit of your home or do it yourself. You are looking for air leaks around windows, doors, the foundation, the roof, and where the walls meet the foundation and the roof.

Be sure to have storm windows/doors if you're in a very cold or very hot climate, or invest in double or triple-glazed windows and good, solid doors. Curtains or shades will add another layer of insulation as well. Caulk any leaky places (there are special weatherization caulks for this purpose).

The best thing to do is to add insulation to your home, especially in the ceiling. That extra layer will keep you warmer in winter and cooler in summer. Insulation is important in any climate. It is possible to retrofit your home to have more insulation. It's best to talk to a professional in these matters: a builder familiar with weatherizing or an energy-efficiency expert. The world of "green" building keeps changing, and the options will be different depending on your current home and your climate. If you seal your home incorrectly, or too tightly, you will have problems with air quality and moisture buildup, so be sure to consult a professional before you do it yourself.

If you plan to move to a smaller home, hold off on insulating your current place but be sure to take care of the leaky places and weatherstrip the windows and doors. (If you are in a rental unit, talk to your landlord about weatherizing.) When you get to your smaller home — either new or old — make sure you have plenty of insulation and good windows.

Some municipalities and utility companies have weatherization programs that may be low or no cost, and some governments provide tax rebates for energy-efficiency up-grades. Check with your state or local officials to find out.

Light frugally

Many electric companies have special deals on compact fluorescent light bulbs (CFLs). Call your utility and find out. CFLs provide as much light as incandescent bulbs at a fraction of the wattage, saving money on your electric bill and decreasing the need to build more power plants.

Some people complain that these bulbs are not bright enough, but it's just that it takes them a little while to come up to full power. Be patient. You can also increase light in a room by having more see-through lampshades (or no lampshade at all) and by situating your lamps in the places where you need and use the direct light.

Keep abreast of the changes in energy-efficient light-ing. CFLs contain mercury (dispose of dead or broken ones at a hazardous-waste collection site), so new bulb types are being developed all the time. There are now halogen and LED lights that rival CFLs in efficiency without the mercury.

You do not need to replace light bulbs in low-use areas such as hallways, closets, the cellar, and the attic. Don't forget the simple step of turning off any lights that are not in use. You may be surprised how this basic act can save you money.

Don't forget natural lighting, either. Our ancestors did not have the gift of electricity. Their light came from the sun in the daytime and from candles, oil lamps, or the central fire in the evening. Make sure that there is no room in your home where you must turn the lights on in the daytime even though the sun is out. Rearrange furniture, cut a few tree limbs, install a larger window — anything to help reduce your need to draw on electricity during the day.

Turn off "phantom loads"

Many of our modern appliances are always on even when we aren't using them. Anything that has a clock is on. Anything that has a remote control is on. Low levels of electricity stream into these appliances so that they are always on the ready to fire up at our command.

Unplug your stereo, TV, VCR, DVD player, computer, printer, microwave, etc. When you want to use them, plug them in. (Or don't use them at all.) You can also choose to plug a group of small appliances or electronic equipment into a power strip and turn that on and off as needed. It'll take just a moment, and you'll see the difference in your electric bill.

Install low-flow showerheads and toilets

The average shower uses gallons and gallons of water. With a low-flow showerhead, easily installed by anyone, you can reduce the amount of water — hot and cold — that you use when you bathe. The quality of these showerheads is excellent, with plenty of water pressure and rinsing ability. They can be found at your local hardware or plumbing store.

You can also consider showering every other day. Unless you are physically active or a hormonally charged adolescent, you may be able to get away with this. It's one simple way to reduce the amount of hot water that you use. Try a quick sponge bath if you think you need it on the days you don't shower.

Consider the other household water hog: the toilet. With each flush, gallons of water go right down the drain. Most new homes come with low-flow toilets. If you don't have them, install them. Or try not flushing with each use. Follow the adage, "If it's yellow, let it mellow; if it's brown, flush it down." Others of you may want to try a composting toilet or more radical, yet safe, ways to dispose of human waste. There are books and websites on the subject; if you're interested, check them out.

Improve your water-heating systems

Hot water uses a great deal of energy in the average household. Whether you have a propane or an electric hot-water heater or one attached to your furnace, you don't need it any hotter than 120°F. Turn it down! Not only will this save you money, it will prevent unintended scalding.

Consider installing an on-demand hot-water heater (which heats water only when you are about to use it) or solar hot-water panels if you have the money and appropriate space (there are often tax credits or rebates for these). If you have a woodstove, you can have a water jacket installed that will allow you to heat hot water when you are running the stove. Talk to your local woodstove dealer about your options.

Try washing (and rinsing) dishes and clothes in cold water. Only the most stubborn grime needs hot water to come clean.

Turn down your heat/turn up your cooling

In the energy crisis of the late 1970s, President Jimmy Carter appeared in a speech to the nation wearing a sweater and encouraged people to turn down the thermostat in order to save on heating fuel. People didn't like hearing that, and it was one of several reasons given for his subsequent defeat for a second term.

But he was right. It makes sense to turn down the thermostat and put on a sweater. A few degrees won't make that much difference to your sense of comfort. If you normally have the thermostat at 72°F during heating season, try 68°. If you're used to 68°, try 65°. Adding a sweater, a pair of slippers, or an undershirt is easy. Or get up and move around if you start to get chilly. During the night, you can get away with setting your thermostat at 50° — that's what blankets are for!

Conversely, unless you live in the hottest of climates, forget the air conditioner and learn to cool your house the way people used to: by opening all the windows at night and closing them (and the curtains) during the day. That will hold in the cooler nighttime air and prevent the daytime heat from coming in. When the sun goes down and the outside temperature cools off, open everything up again.

Use a fan to keep the air moving if there is no breeze.

If you insist on using an air conditioner, try turning up the thermostat. Instead of keeping your house at 72°F, try 75° or 80°, and don't forget to turn it off at night when you open the windows.

You can also consider replacing your heating/cooling system with a newer, more efficient model or even changing the fuel source that you use. It may be expensive to make the change initially, but the money and fuel you save in the long run will be worth it.

Change the way you cook

How many of us love a soup or stew that's simmered all day long on the back of the stove? You don't have to have the heat on under the pot all the time to create the same taste. If you're not in a rush for that pot of soup, try bringing it to a boil, then turn off the heat and let it sit. Do the same thing every couple of hours until it is done. It will be just as tasty and will use much less power to cook. Do the same thing with hard-boiled eggs, dried beans, and grains.

When you do cook dried beans or grains, make a large amount at once and freeze the leftovers. If you're using the oven to bake bread or cookies, be sure to bake as many loaves or pans as fit into your oven at once. Extras will keep for quite a while or can be frozen. If you're baking a casserole or roasting vegetables, throw in some stale bread cubes for croutons, or some granola to toast. Try and do double duty when cooking.

If you live in a sunny climate, you can experiment with cooking in a solar oven. You can make your own oven or purchase one. There are many different kinds of models, whose prices range widely. You can easily cook grains, beans, vegetables, soups, and stews in a solar oven. Give it a try.

Change the way you do laundry

Getting an energy-efficient washing machine is a good idea, if you can afford it. With or without an energy-efficient model, you can save money by washing in cold or warm water instead of hot, using less detergent, doing fewer loads of laundry, and making sure the machine is full (but not too full) when you use it.

Our society has developed a clean fetish. People wear an outfit once, or use a towel once, and into the laundry it goes, whether or not it's really dirty. If you go to work in nice clothes, get into the habit of taking them off as soon as you get home, examining them for true dirtiness (body odor and stains), and changing into home clothes. You can probably get away with the same home outfit for a week or more if you're just wearing it in the evenings, and chances are your work skirts and slacks may only need to be laundered after half a dozen wearings, your shirts and blouses after one or two.

Towels should be hung up to dry after each use. Make sure your home has towel racks or other places available to fully hang out each towel so that it has an opportunity to completely dry: it's the wet towels that get tossed in the corner that need washing frequently. Try changing sheets every other week, or even less often, if you usually do it once a week.

A good rule of thumb is to do no more than one load of dirty clothes per person per week and one load of sheets, towels, and other linens per person per month. If you have a little one in diapers, add in one load of diapers per week. Make a game of this — see just how long an article of clothing can last before it truly needs to be washed.

After you wash, you dry. Dryers, after refrigerators, are the biggest energy hogs in the home. It pays, in more ways than one, to stop using them. Besides, who doesn't like the smell of clothes and linens right off the line? It's time to get rid of your dryer and invest in the old-fashioned way of drying clothes: clothesline and clothespins and/or a sturdy clothes rack. I have never owned a dryer and have successfully hung clothes to dry with babies, toddlers, and teens, with all their various clothing needs.

Clothesline can be strung in a dry basement or attic, on a porch, in a yard between two trees, or between posts you plant in the ground. If your home or yard does not have a place for a clothesline, invest in a clothes rack instead. They can often be found at yard sales, at your local hardware store, or through catalogs. Get a sturdy one that can handle a lifetime of use. One nice thing about clothes racks is that they fold up for easy storage. They can also be used indoors in inclement weather or if you are unfortunate enough to live in a place where hanging laundry outdoors is banned (if that's the case, work on changing that).

Hanging your laundry to dry can be done, in any climate. You just need to plan ahead. No tossing something into the washer and dryer right before you need it: unless you live where it's hot and dry, your clothes will not be ready in time. Keep up with your laundry. When you have enough for one load, run it and then hang it up. Don't forget your children: they love to help with this household job. It takes no more than ten minutes to take down a dry load and hang up a new load — time worth spending.

If you use the laundromat, you can still use a clothes rack or clothesline. Most racks hold at least one load; a clothesline can hold more. To stretch your drying surfaces, hang shirts and tops on hangers on your shower curtain rod. Drape linens over railings, or fences. Be creative. If you tend to wait until all the clothes in the house are dirty before heading out the laundromat, you might want to consider doing the wash when you have just one or two loads so that it's more convenient to air dry them. There's nothing wrong with doing laundry by hand, either. Women all over the world do it every day.

Look at all the rest of your electrical appliances: what do you really need?

Many major appliances come in energy-efficient models. But the most energy-efficient and cost-effective thing to do is not to use them at all.

Take dishwashing. Although there are energy-efficient dishwashers available, it's all relative. A dishwasher of any kind costs you money to buy and uses more hot water than prudent hand washing (using a small amount of water, of any temperature, to wash and being equally frugal with the cold rinse). Another drawback of owning and using a dishwasher is that you need enough dishes to fill it up. If you reduce the amount of unused stuff you own, you might not even have enough dishes to fill it — something that happened to us once when we rented an apartment with a dishwasher. Don't forget the precious space a dishwasher would take up in your smaller home.

Washing dishes can be very relaxing and can provide another opportunity to slow down and pay attention to the gifts that you do have: available clean water coming out of a faucet, dishes, a kitchen, and enough food to eat. It's also an activity that can be done by any member of the family, alone or as a group. It's a great time to talk and get the kitchen cleaned up at the same time.

Then there are microwaves — they are everywhere. Most people consider them indispensable to daily living. Nuke those leftovers, heat up the old coffee, thaw out some meat for dinner, pop some popcorn. The truth is, you don't need a microwave to do any of these things.

Leftovers can be heated up on your stove or eaten cold (or frozen for later use). If you're not fond of leftovers, learn to prepare the exact amount of food you or your family will eat at any one time. Make one cup of coffee or tea at a time or pour the rest of the pot into a thermos to keep hot for the rest of the day. Plan ahead when you want to thaw something out. Buy your popcorn in bulk and pop it in a sturdy pot on the stove, avoiding both the microwave and the excess packaging.

Some people may argue that a microwave uses less electricity to warm leftovers, or pop popcorn, for example, than a conventional stove. That may be true depending on the age, quality, and type of both the microwave and the stove. However, microwave use tends to become habitual and keeps us from looking for another way to do things like planning ahead for thawing out food, eating leftovers cold, or making one cup of coffee at a time. Once upon a time — not that long ago — no one even had a microwave to use, yet people prepared food and beverages without any need to do it so quickly and in such a fashion. If you just adore your microwave and can cook just about anything in it, consider getting rid of your range instead. Why have both?

Look at the rest of your electrical gadgets. Major appliances such as refrigerators and freezers come in energy-efficient versions. If you choose to have these appliances, consider purchasing a smaller, energy-efficient model. You can also find ways to reduce the electricity usage of the ones you do have by keeping the coils on the back of your refrigerator clean, keeping the freezer and refrigerator in a cool location, and keeping the freezer full. Or do without. If you don't freeze your produce or buy locally raised meat in bulk, you probably don't need a chest freezer. Many people in northern climates use the outdoors for refrigeration in the colder months (and understand that many foods do not have to be refrigerated).

Appliances that produce heat use the most electricity — hair dryers, irons, and heating pads, to name just a few. If you have a no-fuss hairstyle, no-fuss clothes, and an old-fashioned hot-water bottle, you will use less electricity and have no need for costly gadgets that take up space. If you do many of your food preparation tasks by hand — kneading bread, beating eggs, chopping vegetables — you won't need all those small appliances to do the work for you. Look at all your electrical gadgets and ask yourself which ones you really need.

Don't forget the electronics you use for entertainment: TV, VCR or DVD player, computer, stereo, radio, iPod, Wii, etc. Part of a frugal life is finding low-cost or no-cost ways to have fun that don't involve electronics or an admission fee (see Chapter Eleven: Fun). You can meet all your electronic entertainment needs through a small laptop computer and access to the Internet. You can watch movies, archives of TV shows, and the latest news. You can livestream radio or listen to music of your choice. By reducing the amount of electronic entertainment you use, and reducing the number of gadgets you own, you'll save money on the purchase and upkeep and on the electric bill (the larger the screen, the higher the energy use) and cable bill, and you'll have lots of extra room in your home if all you need to store is a laptop.

Remember to think twice before you purchase a brand-new large or small appliance, electronic device, or a replacement for one that has died. The best way to save money, energy, and resources is to not own or use the appliance in the first place. If you must have it, consider purchasing a second-hand one.

Get rid of your lawn

Americans are in love with their lawns. A lot of time and money is spent on grooming these green spaces. There is the lawnmower to purchase and maintain, the gas to fuel it, the herbicides and seed to keep the grass perfect, the water to keep it green, and the hours it takes to keep it manicured.

Instead of a lawn that needs to be mowed, plant a vegetable garden, create a wildflower lawn, put in a patio, or design some beautiful flowerbeds. Understand your climate and landscape; don't try and create something that doesn't belong. A rock garden, a wild-grasses garden, a cacti garden: there are many choices. Talk to your local gardening experts to find the best thing to do in your yard.

If you must a have a (small) lawn, choose to share ownership of a gasoline or electric push lawn mower with the neighbors or, better yet, share a human-powered rotary mower. Be sure to mow infrequently and on the highest setting to allow your grass to be healthier and able to withstand high heat and little water.

Don't forget snow removal, another costly addition to home ownership. You don't necessarily need someone to plow for you or an expensive snowblower to purchase, maintain, and run. Unless you have a very long driveway, or live in a very snowy part of the world, hand shoveling is all you'll need to keep your walkways and driveway clear.

Shoveling is great exercise and fun for the kids. If you hate snow removal, try bartering with a friend or neighbor: they shovel for both of you, and you do something in exchange like walk their dog or make them dinner.

Have a rain barrel to catch water

One way to reduce your water bills and save on your water use is to have a rain barrel catching what falls on your roof. You can use the water to nourish your garden or lawn, give to your chickens, or flush your toilets in a pinch. You can find barrels new or used, in wood, metal or plastic. Make sure the barrel is clean and covered to prevent bugs from breeding or small children from getting in trouble. Install it under your downspout, and save that precious water that falls from the sky.

You can also save your "graywater," the water that drains from your sinks, shower, tub, and washing machine. It may be "dirty," but it's clean enough to use to water the garden. You can have a plumber set you up with a graywater catchment system. If you live in a water-scarce place, or a municipality with expensive water and sewer fees, it makes sense.

Consider net metering

Many people now are producing their own electricity and selling it back to their local utility company. You can install solar photovoltaic panels on your south-facing roof, or put up a small wind generator. There is a large cash outlay up front for purchasing and installing this equipment, but you'll end up with no electric bill for many years. Do the math to see if it makes sense for you. You'll also feel good knowing that you are encouraging the use of renewable energy and contributing in a small way to the decrease in carbon emissions into our atmosphere.

Talk to your local utility or a renewable-energy-equipment installer. Everyone has different guidelines for selling power back to the electric company; you'll need to find out what's required in your area. There may also be federal and state rebates for these systems to help defray some of the cost. If you have the money, it's a wise investment.

Learn to "precycle" before you recycle

One great way to reduce trash and recyclables is to not buy products that are in these containers in the first place. Stop buying food in metal, plastic, or glass containers. Learn to buy fresh and skip the plastic bags (or bring your own). To avoid unnecessary packaging, buy your food in bulk or bring your own containers to the bulk section of your health-food store or co-op. Grow your own or purchase vegetables, fruit, herbs, meat, dairy and eggs from a local farmer who will appreciate it if you bring your own containers. Save glass jars and plastic containers that you can't avoid buying, and reuse them to store your bulk foods, leftovers, and brown bag meals.

Learn to refuse packaging and plastic or paper bags at the store (bring your own cloth bags). Return excess packing materials to the company of origin and ask that they reduce the amount of packaging they put on their products. Or buy used — that's one way to avoid all that plastic, Styrofoam, and cardboard. The cost of maintaining current landfills and building new ones affects our trash fees, our property taxes, and our environment. Do what you can to reduce the amount of trash you accumulate.

And always recycle what you can.

Invest in some good-quality reuseable plastic containers and stop buying plastic bags, aluminum foil, etc.

Plastic containers to hold your brown bag lunch, leftover food, and traveling staples are invaluable. You can purchase them, or simply reuse the containers you get at the store that contain yogurt, other dairy products, etc. Be sure to have enough for the whole family if everyone takes a meal to work or school. You can also use them for leftovers, or simply store those leftovers in a bowl with a plate on top in the refrigerator — no need for plastic wrap!

Plastic bags are everywhere, and there is no reason to buy them. If you are in the habit of using store-supplied plastic bags for your produce or your groceries, you can reuse them at home (more than once, if you wash them between uses). Once you learn to reuse plastic bags instead of purchasing them, you can start to take them with you to the store to use once again when you shop. Or you can invest in some lightweight cotton mesh bags designed for fresh produce. Don't forget to bring some large, sturdy cloth bags or a backpack to put your groceries in. That's the answer to "Paper or plastic?"

Use cloth equivalents of paper products

Long before there were paper towels and paper napkins, there were cloth kitchen towels and cloth napkins. Kitchen shops and grocery stores still carry them, so buy some (or make them yourself with scraps of fabric or worn-out bath towels) and stop buying paper. The average kitchen can function well with three or four dishtowels used primarily for drying hands (let those dishes dry by themselves!) when cooking and cleaning. Plan on three cloth napkins per member of your household. Choose some bright and interesting colors and patterns.

For cleaning, invest in some washable cleaning cloths or cloth diapers, or cut up old T-shirts, towels, or sheets and make your own. These can be used for general cleaning and for mopping up the occasional spills and messes (which you might have used paper towels for in the past).

Speaking of diapers, don't let your baby sport disposable diapers. Put them in cloth. They'd thank you if they could. Cloth diapers are friendlier to the environment and to your wallet. They don't take that much time to rinse and wash once you have a system in place. Plastic pants or wool "soakers" handle the protection part. To maintain cleanliness, rinse as soon as possible, and wash and rinse well in hot water (the one exception to the wash-in-cold suggestion). Hang them out to dry in the sunshine: it's the old-fashioned way to help kill any remaining bacteria, and they'll smell good, too.

Many people think that disposable diapers are a necessity. They aren't. We traveled for a month in Europe with a fifteen-month-old in diapers — cloth diapers — and did not find it a hassle. Think how much easier it is at home! Just like anything, it may take you a little while to get a system in place for carrying clean diapers, used diapers, and the appropriate wipes — also known as washcloths. No need for throw-away "baby wipes." Just get yourself a collection of washcloths and always carry at least two (damp and in a plastic bag) with you for on-the-road changes. (Look into a diaper service if you really don't want to handle the diapers yourself.)

Don't forget your handkerchief, either. Before there were disposable "facial tissues," there were hankies — lace-trimmed or plain. You can still buy them at any department store, good men's clothing store, women's lingerie store, or through catalogs or online. Three or four per person is plenty, even when you have a cold (be sure to wash them frequently and in hot water when you're sick).

Finally, for the women, try cloth menstrual pads. You can purchase them readymade with a special snap-in holder, or you can make them yourself out of cloth diapers. Soak after use in a container of water, then rinse and toss in with the rest of your laundry. The soaking water can be used to fertilize your houseplants or garden, or poured down the drain.

Cancel newspaper and magazine subscriptions

Diapers, pads, and paper napkins are not the only disposible paper products we should avoid buying. Books, magazines, and newspapers also use a lot of trees and cost us a lot of money — and time. We can save ourselves some cash, and our planet some trees, by canceling our subscriptions to periodicals and using the library.

Our public libraries are important institutions. Besides providing information and resources, the library is also the community center in many cities and towns. It is important to support our libraries so that they can continue to provide this important service to our community.

Reading is one of the greatest pleasures in life. We are able to learn, understand, explore, and consider new ideas when we read. We can keep current on the day's news. We can do the crossword puzzle or read the comics.

What do you read and where do you get your periodicals? Are you used to reaching for the morning paper as you pour that first cup of coffee? Would you feel lost without knowing the headlines or chuckling over your favorite comic strip before you leave the house? Or do the papers pile up, unread, for days? Do you have stacks of unread magazines that you subscribed to at some point for some reason? Or do you subscribe to magazines that you sit down with as soon as they arrive?

Try this: cancel all your current newspaper and magazine subscriptions, or, if you can't go cold turkey, wait until they expire and don't renew. See what it feels like to go without. You will probably feel some degree of relief that unread periodicals are not taking up space in your living room, beside your bed, or in the recycling bin. If you find you miss a particular magazine, head to your local library and see if they have it. If they don't, you can ask them to get it, or purchase a subscription for them as a gift.

As for the morning news, there are many ways to get it without destroying so many trees and spending so much money. You can tune in to your favorite radio station at home or in the car. You can log on to any major news media website if you have a computer and Internet access. Or you can do without. Many people suggest that the news is contributing to our stress level. Try taking a news vacation and see how you feel.

For those of you who get the paper for the crossword puzzle, the chess column, or the comics, you can head to the library once a week to catch up on those. Or, in many cases, you can find them on the Internet.

Cancel catalogues and junk mail

Don't just toss those unwanted catalogs and requests for money in the recycling bin; contact the business and get your name off their list. For catalog companies, just call their toll-free number and ask to be removed. For nonprofits and other organizations that solicit your donation by mail, either mark the envelope "refused, return to sender" or write on the donation slip "please remove me from your mailing list," put it in their envelope, and mail. Be sure to indicate to any organization or business that you do support that you do not want them selling or giving your name to anyone else.

Do the same thing with unwanted e-mails from companies trying to sell you their products, or nonprofits asking you to donate or sign petitions. Any reputable business or organization will have an "unsubscribe" feature on these e-mails. Use it. These e-mails don't destroy trees or cost you money, but they can be annoying and waste your precious time and bandwidth.

Pay your bills electronically

Many utilities, local governments, and other businesses allow you to pay your bills electronically. This service allows the business to transfer the money you owe directly from your savings or checking account to their account. The businesses do this with your written permission only, and they will send you a bill first (on paper or via e-mail) with a date when the transfer will be made, so you can plan ahead. If everyone took advantage of this service, we would save countless trees and have less paper to recycle. It saves time and the cost of postage, and you'll never have to worry about late fees.

Use scrap paper

Save sheets of paper with writing only on one side to use as scrap paper. They're handy for printing documents that won't be seen by other people, making shopping and to-do lists, drawing pictures, cutting out snowflakes, and writing the first draft of a letter, essay, or story. Keep a pile by the phone, in the kitchen, and by the printer.

Save your holiday and birthday wrapping paper, too, for reuse on other special occasions. If you're careful when you unwrap a gift, you can easily fold and store the paper for another time. If you run out of wrapping paper, use newspaper, scrap paper drawings, or pieces of fabric.

Purchase paper only when absolutely necessary, and look for paper made from recycled post-consumer waste when you do.

Start a compost pile

A large percentage of our garbage is food scraps that can be composted. Unless you live deep in the heart of a major city, you can have a compost pile in your backyard or a friend's backyard. If you are in a big city, you can experiment with a worm-composting unit under your sink, save your scraps for a friend who composts, or participate in your city's food-waste recycling program. You can also make wonderful vegetable stocks with carrot and celery tops, onion skins, and other vegetable scraps before you get rid of them. Just collect them in a pot while you're preparing dinner, cover with water, bring to a boil, and let sit for an hour or so. Once the stock is done, drain and chuck the scraps into the compost.

Save all your food scraps — fruit and vegetable ends and peels, coffee grounds, tea bags, and eggshells — and deposit them, along with other organic materials such as leaves or seaweed, into your backyard bin. (Avoid any animal flesh or dairy products: they attract unwanted critters.) You can build a bin with two-by-fours or short lengths of small trees, or you can purchase a special bin from a gardening store or catalog. Most any organic-gardening book should have a section on making compost;

go to your local library and look one over for complete instructions.

Compost piles don't have to smell bad, bother the neighbors, or be a fast-food joint for local animals. Follow the instructions and you will have wonderful organic fertilizer for your outdoor garden or plants in pots.

Don't forget to eat your leftovers for lunch the next day, or learn to serve just the amount you and your family will eat at meals — no more scraping plates into the trash. Encourage your local schools and hospitals to start composting as well. You can also get some chickens; they'll love to eat your scraps, and they'll turn them into compost for you.

Before you throw anything out, ask if it can be repaired, used for another purpose, or given away

Turn a critical eye to everything headed for the trash. Could someone else get some use out of this? Are there spare parts that could be used? Could the clothes be turned into rags, given to Goodwill, or used for quilts or rugs? Can the item be repaired? Can the broken pottery pieces be used for drainage at the bottom of houseplants?

But don't hold onto stuff just because you think it's wrong to throw it away. It'll just become clutter in your home and will take up valuable space. Join the Freecycle Network™, an online organization where you can offer your unneeded items to others who could use them (plus you can ask for things you may need). Freecycle groups are available worldwide; just go to www.freecycle.org to sign up for a group in your area. Or leave it out in front of your house with a "free" sign, and someone may take it away. One person's trash is another person's treasure.

Use fewer cleaning products

Our world is inundated with products that promise a whiter white and a brighter shine. Is that really necessary? For centuries, people have kept their homes and belongings clean with the simple materials of soap, water, and elbow grease. You can, too.

There are all kinds of nontoxic, environmentally friendly cleaning products on the market today, but they are expensive. You can make your own cleaning products simply and inexpensively with baking soda, white vinegar, and Borax. There are books on how to do this; check your library.

If you're not ready for that step, you can easily limit your cleaning products to one powdered cleanser, one all-purpose cleaning spray, and a bottle of plain ammonia. If you have a broom and a dustpan and some cleaning cloths or rags, you're all set to tidy up your house.

Laundry soap is all we need for the wash. Dish soap is all we need for dishes. Experiment with using less soap each time you do dishes (by hand!) or do the laundry. Manufacturers want us to use their products. See how little you can get away with. If you do your laundry less often, you'll use even less soap (along with water and electricity). If you spend a lot of time (and money) using bleach or stain removers on your clothes, perhaps you might consider having clothes that don't require special treatment. Forget the dazzling white shirts and head for a more practical color. Don't forget to use your cloth napkin to avoid food stains!

Streamline your house cleaning

Speaking of cleaning, you don't need to spend hours on your day off cleaning the house (or hiring someone else to do it because you're too tired). The average home can be cleaned easily by two people in an hour, or four in a half hour. That's another good reason to have a smaller, rather than larger, home.

Housecleaning should be shared by all members of the family, and children are never too young to learn. If they can walk and hold a dustpan, they can help. Divide up the areas to be cleaned — generally that's the bathroom(s), the kitchen, the dusting, and the floors. Assign one area to each family member (if there are four of you), or have two people divvy the jobs up. If you have three or five in your family, you do the math! People can stay with one job if they prefer it, or you can plan on rotating.

If everyone works together, the job will be done faster and there will be more time for everyone to pursue his or her own interests. If working together won't fit into your schedule, break the jobs into smaller pieces — one or two things per day — and divide them up equally among your household members. Save the big cleaning jobs like washing windows for once or twice a year on a nice day when everyone will want to be outside.

Check out *Speed Cleaning* (Jeff Campbell and the Clean Team, Random House, 1991) for all the details of how to clean your house quickly and efficiently.

Get rid of your cellphone or your home phone

It's an electronic, connected world. It seems like just about everyone has a cellphone and can't imagine life without it. How did we function without being able to reach each other instantly? Our society grows impatient if someone or something is not available to them ASAP.

Look at what you're paying to have both cellphone and landline coverage. It's probably at least a hundred dollars a month, depending on your location, utility company, and usage. Don't forget to consider the purchase price of both cellphones and home phones, and the hidden cost of manufacture and disposal.

Having a telephone is a wonderful convenience that we all take for granted. By all means have a phone, but have one or the other. If every family member in your household insists on a cellphone, then get rid of your landline. Better yet, ditch those cellphones. Free yourself from the tyranny of being available at every second.

While you're looking at your phone usage, be sure to have a local and long-distance calling plan that most appropriately fits your needs. Shop around for the best price. Consider using Skype or another Internet-based phone service. The technology and services keep changing, so you'll need to keep up with all the options to get the best price for your needs.

Decorate/redecorate in a frugal way

We all want our homes to feel cozy and look nice. However, we don't have to have top-of-the line furnishings or the services of an interior decorator to get that.

One of the most inexpensive ways to change or cheer up living space is with a fresh coat of paint. You can buy new paint or scout yard sales for partial cans of used paint and be creative with color and design.

You can find all kinds of quality used furniture at yard sales, thrift shops, and online. Or repaint, recover, and repair the furniture you have. New curtains (that you make yourself) will brighten up or improve an otherwise boring space.

Use your imagination and your creativity when you want to change the look in your home. Sometimes moving the furniture around is enough. Experiment and find an inexpensive solution that works for you.

Keep up with maintenance

Above all, take care of your home and your belongings. Don't defer repairs — major or minor — that will end up costing more in the long run if they aren't attended to. Create a plan for regular maintenance: how often you need to clean your chimney or your furnace, check your roof for leaks, check the siding for the next paint job, inspect the foundation for cracks, etc. Keep up with maintenance on your furnishings and appliances as well. Oil things that need to be oiled, repair broken furniture before someone gets hurt, fix a leaky faucet before your water bill escalates.

Owning a home, and the things inside that make it a home, is a responsibility. But whether you rent or own, take care of what you have. In the long haul, you'll save both time and money.

7. Food

We need food to sustain life. Nutritious food and clean water are even more necessary than shelter. Buying, growing, preserving, cooking, eating, and cleaning up after food takes a big chunk of our time and our money. Many people resort to fast food, takeout, microwavable meals, and other expensive and not very healthy ways to fill their bellies.

We can eat well, and easily, for less. We can learn how to plan ahead, how to cook, and how to make food a more joyful part of our lives. Since eating is a requirement for living, why not make it as interesting as possible? The new food preparation and consumption habits you will learn will take you anywhere you want to go. Things will taste better, you will feel better, and you will spend less money.

Here are some ways to cut costs and improve the quality of the food you eat.

Know what your food costs you

To be able to learn how to spend less on food (without sacrificing flavor and nutrition), you'll need to know what you currently spend. As you keep track of your expenses, divide your food purchases into what you buy at the grocery store or food co-op, what you buy at convenience stores, and what you buy at restaurants or fast-food places. Don't forget to include the farmer's market or food bought directly from the grower. If you have a vegetable garden, keep track of what you spend on seeds, plants, and soil amendments. If you keep chickens or other livestock, include their expenses as well.

As you look at your receipts, be sure to take out nonfood items that you purchase when you're buying food — cleaning supplies, toilet paper, etc. — and have a separate category for what you spend on alcohol.

Once you know what you're spending on food, and where you're spending it, you'll be able to figure out how you can reduce costs and increase quality with the following suggestions.

Eat foods in season

Learn what foods grow in your area, and when. Some foods are grown all year, and others have a limited season. When your supermarket offers strawberries in January, and in your state they don't start being harvested until May, you know you'll be eating a tasteless and expensive berry that came from very far away.

There are cold-weather crops and hot-weather crops. We all know the difference in flavor and price of the December tomato versus the July tomato, the June apple versus the October apple, the February green bean versus the August green bean. Enjoy each fruit and vegetable in its season, knowing that the cycle of the year will repeat itself and you'll get to have it fresh once again.

Many staple vegetables such as potatoes, onions, and carrots are available all year round at a consistent price and flavor. Improved storage facilities and greenhouses have lengthened the season for many fruits and vegetables, and we should take advantage of that. But we'll never eat fresh and inexpensive cucumbers every month of the year.

If you start eating a majority of plant foods, you'll want to eat them when they are freshest and cheapest. Keep your eyes open as you shop, talk to the produce manager of your favorite store, and avoid buying those January strawberries, as tempting as they may be.

If you really crave a fruit or vegetable out of season, check the frozen produce department. The prices and quality are often better.

Eat humanely raised animal products

Although pasture-raised cows, sheep, pigs, and poultry and sustainably harvested fish cost more than factory-farmed animal products available at the grocery store, this is one place where it's frugal to spend more for your food. People tend to consume too much meat (usually in the form of fast food and processed food), so spending more at the outset and using less at your meals will balance out, price-wise. Think of these flavor- and nutrient-rich foods as condiments, rather than the centerpieces of your meals. Forget the ten-ounce steaks, and add smaller amounts of animal protein to your seasonal-produce-based stir-frys, stews, salads, and sauces.

Factory-farmed animals may cost less at the checkout, but they are costing us far too much in terms of the resources used to raise them (water, antibiotics, fossil-fuel-derived pesticides and herbicides that are used to grow their feed, etc.), the food-borne illnesses that come from the crowded conditions at feed lots, and unsanitary conditions at slaughterhouses. Locally grown meats may cost a little bit more, but since you'll be eating less of them, it won't make a dent in your budget. If you buy them in bulk — a quarter or half an animal or a dozen chickens, for example — it will cost even less. If you have the space and really want to understand where your meat comes from, try raising a few chickens or a pig.

If you are a vegetarian or a vegan, that's your choice, but nutrient-rich, sustainably raised animal products may be better for you than excessive amounts of grains and soy products. For an eye-opening account of the realities of these issues, read *The Vegetarian Myth* (Lierre Keith, Flashpoint Press/PM Press, 2009). Check out www.eatwild.com for a listing of farmers who raise these products and have them available for sale directly to the consumer for a reasonable price.

Make friends with a farmer

If you want wonderful foods in season, it's best to get them locally. With the rise of the local-foods movement, many farmers are turning to growing a wide variety of produce. Take advantage of this.

You can buy a share in a Community Supported Agriculture (CSA) program. Sometime during the winter months, you pay a farmer of your choice a certain amount of money to receive fresh foods on a regular basis during your growing season. Most CSAs offer fresh produce; others also offer herbs, flowers, legumes, nuts, grains, breads, meats, dairy products, and eggs. Find out what's available in your area.

Your CSA farmer may also offer pick-your-own days when an abundance of a certain crop or the threat of a frost makes them open their farm for you to help yourself. You can show up and harvest peas, beans, peppers, cucumbers, basil, or what-have-you for little or no cost. Some farmers allow you to work on the farm in exchange for the cost of the CSA share. It's a great way to learn more about your food and where it comes from.

Some farmers don't offer a CSA program, but may have a farm stand, a booth at your farmer's market, or another way to buy their products. If you develop a relationship with them, you will also have an opportunity to learn more about where your food comes from and the chance to get inexpensive or free food when they are overwhelmed with a particular crop.

Making friends with a farmer is also a form of insurance. Someday, when the cost of transporting food over great distances becomes prohibitive, you and your neighbors won't go hungry. Farmers are a vital part of your local economy, and they help to keep the landscape open.

Watch your portions

Many Americans simply consume too many calories, and that costs money. Keep track of what you eat for several days, and calculate the calorie count. This is not to diet or to lose weight, but simply to see where your calories are coming from, and how many you're consuming. Adults and children alike are spending too much time sitting around and eating too many high-sugar, high-fat, and low-nutrient foods. That's costing both your health and your pocketbook.

What are you eating, and how much? Experts disagree on exactly how many calories the average adult man and woman need, but the general consensus is if you are eating more than 2,500 calories a day (men) and 2,000 (women), it's probably too much.

Simplify your meals

Whoever said you must have a balanced meal every time you sit down to eat was wrong. You need to eat, and you need to eat fresh, whole foods. Dinner does not have to include meat, potatoes, vegetables, and dessert. Breakfast does not have to be eggs, bacon, toast, and juice. Food is food: there's no hard and fast rule about what to eat at each meal.

If you're eating seasonally, your meals will revolve around what's available. You can focus each meal on the fresh produce you have, with grains, legumes, meat, and dairy as extras. If you're a traditionalist, have eggs and toast for breakfast, or try yogurt and fruit. Now and then, switch things around and have these foods for dinner. Soups, salads, and stir-frys are good at any meal. A bowl of popcorn, a wedge of cheese, and some fresh fruit will suffice for a meal at any time of day.

Now is the time to toss away assumptions and the latest fad diet. Fresh, seasonal foods are best — for any body. Eat what you love, with pleasure and good company. You don't have to turn mealtime into a big production: be creative. Start with fruits and vegetables and go from there.

Stop buying packaged and prepared foods: learn to cook

Packaged foods — rice mixes, processed cereals, sweets, canned soups, bottled juice, pasta sauce, and condiments of all kinds — are more expensive and less healthy, and cause more trash for our overburdened landfills than those made from scratch. You can purchase vinegar, olive oil, vegetable oil, honey, fresh produce, and herbs and make your own salad dressings, salsas, chutneys, ketchup, mustard, and a variety of sauces.

Choose your favorite condiment or specialty food (bread, pastries, mustard, and salsa come to mind) and learn to make it yourself. You can get recipes everywhere — in cookbooks, on the Internet, and from friends. If you have a friend who's a good cook, ask him or her to teach you. It can be fun and creative to learn how to do this, and, in addition to all the money you'll save by cooking from scratch, you'll save on your trash and recycling bill, since you won't have all that packaging to dispose of.

You can also learn to make such basic foods as soups, stews, casseroles, and pasta sauces from raw ingredients. It just takes practice and planning ahead. You can make extras to keep in your freezer, and you'll never need to buy another can of soup or jar of spaghetti sauce just to have on hand for drop-in visitors or a night when you don't want to cook.

Homemade salad dressings are simple and inexpensive to make. Equal parts olive or vegetable oil with vinegar or lemon juice is a good place to start. Add chopped garlic or onion, prepared or dry mustard, herbs of your choice, and you're all set. Try adding some of your favorite cheese (blue or not) or honey and tomato juice for a zesty dressing. A blender will make a smooth dressing, but finely chopped or grated ingredients will shake up just fine with the oil and vinegar in a jar.

One reason people turn to prepared or fast foods instead of cooking from scratch is that it's faster. Learn to have basic foods already prepared and waiting for hungry people. Have salad greens and vegetables washed, cut up, and properly stored so people can throw together a salad in seconds (don't forget to have a selection of dressings prepared as well). Slice or grate cheese instead of paying the manufacturer to do it for you. Keep hard-boiled eggs on hand if your family eats them on a regular basis. Have garlic cloves peeled and stored in a jar in the fridge. Soak and cook a large quantity of your favorite legumes now and then, and freeze them in small, usable quantities. Choose a regular time each week to be your own prep cook, and you'll save both time and money.

If you love to cook, experiment! Don't get hung up on recipes and fancy, out-of-season, and expensive ingredients. As the saying goes, "Eat local, spice global." Experiment with a variety of international spices and see what you like (be sure to buy those spices in bulk at your health-food store or food co-op: they'll be a fraction of the price — and fresher — than the ones from the grocery store). If you don't really like to cook, find ways to create satisfying meals simply. Anyone can chop vegetables and stir-fry or steam them, wash salad greens, make pasta or rice, and slice cheese. Don't forget to involve your whole family: the best cooks in the house may be younger than you are.

Food should be pleasurable, not stressful. Keep that in mind as you prepare and enjoy your meals. If you really, really hate to cook, enlist a friend to cook for you, preparing soups, stews, and casseroles for the freezer, and do something for them that they'd rather not do.

Buy food in bulk

I'm not talking about buying a case of potato chips in four-ounce bags, or a twelve-pack of soda! Over time, as you start cooking from scratch, you will gain a better sense of what raw ingredients your family uses. You may even know just how much rice, olive oil, pinto beans, pasta, or honey you use in a month or a year.

It's time to buy in bulk. It may seem scary to buy a fifty-pound bag of rice, but if there are four of you and you eat rice once or twice a week, you'll be through the bag in no time. Be sure to have a clean, dry place to store your bulk purchases. Three-gallon plastic pails with tight-fitting lids are often available from food co-ops, health-food stores, or bulk-buying groups, and they work well for bulk purchases. Generally, twenty-five pounds of a dry food fits into a three-gallon pail.

There are many places to buy food in bulk. Some communities have special bulk-only grocery stores. Don't be pulled in by the junk food in bulk; look for grains, legumes, nuts, peanut butter, canned tomatoes, oils, vinegars, coffee, and tea. You can also ask to order in bulk at your food co-op or health-food store, or you can look for a preorder bulk-buying group that usually uses the same wholesale supplier as the health-food store or co-op and is much cheaper. In some cases, you can buy in bulk directly from a farmer who grows the legumes, grains, or nuts.

Buying in bulk saves you money, it saves on packaging that eventually has to be thrown away or recycled, and it saves you trips to the store. You will always have extra food on hand for company, when no one feels like shopping, or when a big storm keeps you home. After a while, you will learn just how much food your family uses in a year, making it that much easier to plan ahead and purchase those ingredients when they are on sale.

Many of today's kitchens don't have the traditional pantry space our grandmothers knew. You may find that your cupboard shelves are not tall enough for gallon jars or large containers. Save smaller containers in which to put your bulk purchases (no need to buy fancy jars!), and then store the original, larger containers in another room or closet if there's no place in the kitchen. Before long, you'll wonder why you never shopped this way before.

Know what's in your refrigerator, freezer, pantry, and cupboards

Be aware of the food that's in your house. Too many people throw out too much food because it gets buried in the back of the refrigerator or cupboard and goes bad. Learn to plan ahead, eat what you have, and keep your staple foods well stocked. It will cost you less in time and money if you don't have to run out at the last minute for a key ingredient, if you learn to eat what you have before you buy more, and if you are careful not to let food go bad.

It makes sense to have a selection of the staple foods your family uses always on hand. This can be a selection of grains (rice, pasta, cornmeal, oats, flour, etc.), legumes (split peas, lentils, white beans, etc.), oils (olive, sunflower, etc.), vinegar (cider, wine, balsamic, etc.), herbs and spices, baking powder and baking soda, sweeteners (sugar, honey, maple syrup, etc.), nuts, and nut butters. With whatever fresh, canned, or frozen produce you have, you will always be able to put together a meal.

If you have a cupboard full of all kinds of foods you rarely use and didn't even know you had, try an experiment. Eat it all up without purchasing anything new. This is a great way to save a significant amount of money right away while cleaning out your cupboards at the same time. Be creative: you may live primarily on funny casseroles and weird soups for a little while, but it will give you much food for thought. People living in poverty, in war-torn areas, or in places affected by natural disasters don't have the food choices that we do. If you spend time eating just what you have, you'll start to understand what it's like for people who have no choice. And once you've eaten up what you've got and start to choose again, you'll be that much more appreciative of what you do have.

By becoming aware of the foods you have and use on a regular basis, you will also learn how to make substitutions in recipes, how to throw together a meal with what you have that's on the edge of spoiling, and how to stock up on needed items through your bulk-buying group or when they are on sale.

Cut back on junk food and soft drinks

You know it's bad for you, and junk food is also incredibly expensive in many other ways. There is a steep environmental cost from highly packaged, low-nutrient foods: our roadsides, landfills, and cars are littered with the evidence. There is a health cost as people gain more weight every year, much of it from high-fat, high-sugar junk food and lack of exercise. There is a financial cost as well. Why pay several dollars for a pound of potatoes as chips when you can buy a pound of the real thing for pennies? Then you can prepare them any way you want them — chips included.

Chips, soda, specialty juices and drinks, cupcakes, cookies, crackers, candy — the list goes on and on. Say no to junk food. Remember to carry your own bottle of water from home, or a thermos of your favorite hot beverage. Don't leave the house without some dried fruit, nuts, a sandwich, or some cheese in case you get hungry along the way. Plan ahead, and you won't be tempted. Stops at convenience stores will become a thing of the past. Think of the time and money (and trash) you'll save.

But wait! What about the kids? Won't their friends expect chips and dip, sodas, and microwave pizza when they come over? Maybe, but that's no reason to waste your hard-earned money. Homemade cookies (especially if the kids make them), freshly popped popcorn, or quesadillas straight from the broiler will please any young people hanging out at your house. And there's nothing like water or a glass of milk to wash it all down. (If you're concerned about the quality of your tap water, invest in a water filter and forget about buying fancy water in plastic bottles.)

Rethink your relationship with coffee and tea

Most of us wouldn't dream of doing without our morning cup of coffee or tea. But this habit can cost us a lot of money. How many times do we make a whole pot of coffee and only drink one cup? How many times are we in such a rush that we stop at the local coffee shop or convenience store for our daily jolt of caffeine? How many of us get queasy or burning stomachs from too much of a tasty thing? How many disposable coffee cups litter our cars, our offices, and our homes? How much money do you spend on coffee and tea?

Coffee and tea are special foods, but they're not always good for us, and they come long distances to reach us. Perhaps you would cut down on your coffee and tea consumption for the money you'll save — and more.

If you can't imagine doing without, consider drinking one cup a day of high-quality, sustainably grown coffee or tea. Take the time to prepare it just the way you like it and savor it. If you want coffee or tea on the road, fill up your thermos before you leave home. Make your own iced tea by filling a jar with water and adding a tea bag or two (or a couple of spoonfuls of loose tea) and letting it steep on the counter for a few hours.

Substitute herb tea (peppermint, chamomile, and rose hips are good and inexpensive choices) or hot water and lemon when you're in the mood for a warming pick-me-up. You can turn the same ingredients into iced drinks for hot weather as well. Don't forget plain tap water. It's always refreshing and the most inexpensive thing you can drink.

While you're at it, reduce other expensive and raised-far-away foods. Unless you live near a banana or mango farm, reduce these, and other, tropical foods from your diet. Same goes for chocolate (I can hear the screams now). As with coffee and tea, if you choose to eat a few of these foods as a treat, be sure to choose sustainably raised products.

Cut down on eating out and learn to brown-bag it

This may challenge you! In our busy world, many people rely on fast food or takeout to supply lunch or dinner. Many people enjoy an evening out at a restaurant as a way to relax and spend time with their spouse or their friends. Workers have given up on bringing food from home, and run to the corner deli for a sandwich or get lunch from a vending machine. Some people think that fast food is a good buy and an economical way to feed a hungry family at the end of a long day. It's not.

Homemade hamburgers are cheaper and healthier than those found at your favorite drive-through. Saving some leftover dinner for lunch the next day or throwing together a peanut-butter sandwich and sticking it in your briefcase is quick and easy. It's also a fraction of the cost of that purchased meal.

Think about the occasions when you rely on buying prepared foods: on the road (with cranky kids, or a cranky you), after a long day at work, for a special event, or when you're in the mood for Chinese and you have no vegetables in the house. Paying someone else to prepare food for you is expensive and not always satisfying.

Learn to plan ahead. Pack your lunch the night before, or plan to take a container with dinner leftovers. Travel with food and beverages in your car or in your purse or briefcase. Nuts, dried fruit, bread, and cheese are quick and easy. Learn to fill a water bottle, travel mug, or small thermos when you leave the house or office. If you are always too exhausted to cook, find some other cooks in your household. Any child over ten can prepare a nice dinner, and the ones under ten can at least put a cheese sandwich, scrambled eggs, or a bowl of cereal on the table for everyone. Find some creative solutions that work for you.

By all means, go out to eat at a restaurant now and then. Dress up, ask one or more of your favorite people, and really enjoy yourself. Choose a restaurant that features seasonal and locally grown foods. Treat eating out as the treat it is meant to be.

Grow a few food plants in pots, or start a small garden

If you have never gardened or are in a location without a suitable yard for a garden, try growing some food plants in pots. Tomato and pepper plants are a good place to start. Common kitchen herbs such as basil, oregano, and dill also grow beautifully in small pots, indoors or out.

Once you become comfortable with growing started plants (such as tomatoes, peppers, eggplant, broccoli, or Brussels sprouts), you can try your hand at container gardening from seed. Lettuce, spinach, and other greens grow nicely in pots, as do zucchini and cucumbers. You can use traditional houseplant pots for your vegetables, or more creative and "make do" pots such as plastic buckets or small wooden barrels filled with potting soil and compost.

Many people prefer container gardening to traditional gardening, as there are fewer weeds and you don't have to bend over as far to care for your plants. If you're in the city with a small balcony, porch, or deck, you can probably grow all of your fresh tomatoes and a good share of other produce as well.

You can even grow fruit in containers. Try a few strawberry plants, or a dwarf lemon or orange tree. Speak to the people at your local garden center for advice on container gardening, or check out a book from the library.

When you're ready, and if you have the space, you can turn your whole yard into a garden. You'll just need a few hand tools and some nicely rotted compost to grow a multitude of vegetables, herbs, and fruit. If you don't have the space, look to your town or city's community garden program, or enlist the help of a friend with a big yard.

Use edible landscaping

Fruit and vegetable plants are often more attractive than ornamental flowers and shrubs. Let your plantings do double duty — food plus beauty. Blueberry bushes' leaves turn an attractive deep red after a frost. Squash blossoms are showy (and dipped in batter and fried, they are a tasty meal). Fruit and nut trees provide beautiful and aromatic spring flowers. Multicolored herbs and vegetables provide contrast to an otherwise boring yard.

Before you plant that cedar hedge, or those flowering shrubs, look to some ordinary, yet beautiful, fruits and vegetables. There are many good books on the subject; check them out at your local library.

Learn to preserve your own food

When those blueberry bushes are heavily laden with fruit, you'll want to learn how to save some for later. When your tomatoes or zucchini seem to take over — or if they're cheap at the market — it's nice to know that by drying, canning, or freezing, you'll be able to eat them next winter. Even if you don't have an overflowing garden, you can often buy bushels of tomatoes, apples, cucumbers, and other fruits and vegetables from your local farmers to turn into tasty meals at a later date.

Bags of carrots, onions, potatoes, and other root crops can be kept easily in a cool closet or cellar. You can turn cabbage into sauerkraut, if you like it, or you can just keep the heads in a cool, dry place. Winter squash will store on a shelf in a dark, cool corner. If you have a root cellar, all the better, but you don't need one to successfully store these crops. Herbs, fruits, and vegetables can be dried without any special equipment. Freezing can also be done easily if you have freezer space. Canning does require purchasing a canner and jars, but you can make small batches of pickles, chutneys, salsas, jams, and jellies, and refrigerate them without needing to process them in a canner.

To find out more about canning, drying, and freezing, look for a class or information about food preservation from your county Extension Service, a community college or adult-learning center, or a nearby farm. There are many books on the subject; my favorite is *Putting Food By* (Janet Greene, Plume, 1992).

Learn about wild foods

Every place has wild foods — city, country, or suburbs. You probably have a salad growing in your yard, or in the empty lot down the street. Many different kinds of mushrooms, berries, nuts, roots, and flowers are edible, be they wild or cultivated. Learn what you can eat for free in your area. Look for a book, a class, or a friend who has experience finding and identifying wild foods. Some are poisonous, or not very tasty. Others need to be prepared in a certain way, or harvested at a certain time of year to taste good and be safe. Learn from an expert. If you're in a city, you also need to be aware that some areas may be contaminated with lead or other heavy metals, so use common sense when harvesting wild foods in an urban environment.

There may also be cultivated foods in your neighborhood you can harvest for free. Many people have mature fruit or nut trees or too many berry bushes to contend with. As you walk around your town, keep your eyes open. Chances are, the owner of the bushes or the trees would be happy for you to harvest the bounty. They won't have to clean up the mess on the lawn, or feel guilty that they aren't eating it all themselves. It's a win-win solution for everyone, especially if you bring them some homemade jam in thanks.

Experiment with limiting your food spending in line with governmental assistance

Another fun and enlightening thing to do to help you learn more about food, cooking, and cutting costs is to try to keep your food budget — for a week or a month — in line with what the government gives people who qualify for Food Stamps (now known as the Supplemental Nutrition Assistance Program). Check their website, www.fns.usda.gov, for the current benefit amounts.

Engage your children in this activity. Talk about food, where it comes from, how much it costs, about the effects of hunger on health and well-being, and what it might be like not to have enough food on the table. You and your family will gain a greater appreciation of the plight of billions in our world, some of whom may be your neighbors or even you at some point in your life.

This experiment may also bring you long-term financial benefits. You may learn ways to eat well for even less money than you thought possible, while gaining a greater appreciation and sense of compassion for those who go hungry every day.

8. Transportation

We need to be able to get from place to place in some way, and most of us feel that we could not possibly give up our car or truck, no matter how much it costs to use. We drive to work, to the store, to a concert, to the movies, to the sports arena, and to visit friends. If we need to pick up something, it's only a drive away.

But, if we want to save money, though not necessarily our time, we need to change our habits, and that takes practice, some ingenuity, and planning ahead. More than once on a rainy day, I've wanted to hop in the car for a quick trip to the grocery store. Instead, I've grabbed an umbrella and a backpack or the shopping cart and headed to the store on foot. It can be lovely to take a walk in the rain.

You may not like walking in the rain, but spending extensive time in the car is not that much fun either. You have to deal with traffic, road construction, bad weather, flat tires, and mechanical problems. Then there's the expense: fuel, registration, insurance, maintenance, and repairs, plus the cost of the vehicle. These things are only going to go up in price as time goes on.

See if you can cut back on driving (and other fossil-fuel-based methods of transportation) and learn to get around in different and more frugal ways. Here are some ideas.

Keep track of your miles driven and your miles per gallon

Before you can start saving money on your vehicle use, it helps to know just how much you're using your car(s) or truck(s) and what they are costing you. It's time to keep track. If you have kids old enough to read and write, have them help you.

Each time you use the car for the next month, write down your start and end mileage and what you did on that trip — buy groceries, take your children to school, commute to work, visit friends. Include how much time the trip took. Write down the amount of gas (and the amount of dollars paid) each time you buy fuel, and what the mileage was, and with each fill-up calculate your miles per gallon. At the end of the month, calculate how many miles you've driven, how much time you've spent on the road, and how much money you've spent for that privilege.

If you continue to keep track as you cut back on driving, you will see how much money you're saving, and whether you can also improve on your miles per gallon.

While you're keeping track of fuel costs, also calculate what you pay in parking, registration, insurance, upkeep, speeding tickets, car payments, and public transportation.

Drive less

This is the obvious solution to save money and wear-and-tear on your vehicle, but may take some creative thinking depending on where you live, what kind of work you do, if you have children, and everyone's interests and activities. You may be in an area with little or no public transportation. Your public transportation may go through areas of your city that feel dangerous to you. Or public transportation may not be convenient to your neighborhood.

Driving is more "convenient" than public transportation, carpooling, walking, or biking. You have to plan ahead if you're getting around by one of these alternative forms of transportation. Once you're in the habit, though, it becomes less of a problem. And by taking public transportation, walking, or biking, you'll not only be saving money, you'll be getting more exercise and you'll be cutting down on the environmental consequences of driving.

Walk more

Walking is one of the best forms of exercise there is, and it's free. If you live a mile or less from basic services, you can do everything on foot. Walk to the store, to the library, to the movies, to the theater, to the ballpark, to church or temple, or to visit friends.

If you live in the country, where walking can often be out of the question, or if you live too far from services and you have no choice but to use a car to do all these things, be sure to consolidate your trips. Keep a list of all the things you need to do in town, and make an afternoon or a day of it once every week or two.

Get a good bike and bike cart or wheeled shopping cart

If you prefer, you can bike instead of walk. Riding a bike allows you to go further and carry heavier loads than walking does. To be able to shop or commute on a bike, you need to have a sturdy, comfortable bike. Go to a good bike shop and explain what you need the bike for. There are many models and types, so be sure to choose the right one. If you are already knowledgeable about bikes, you can easily find the right used bike on your own. Many bike shops have bike swaps once a year, so ask around.

If you plan to grocery shop without your car, you'll need a bike cart for your bike, or a wheeled shopping cart if you're on foot (this can be found at your local hardware store for a modest price). Both carts can carry at least four large paper sacks of food (but bring your own bags). Either cart also comes in handy for hauling other items and is well worth the investment. Have a sturdy backpack for those times when you don't need to carry so much stuff.

Be sure to have a raincoat or poncho and rain pants for those times when inclement weather hits. Don't forget a helmet, a horn, and a light. And if your city or town doesn't have safe bike paths and sidewalks, lobby the appropriate authorities to see if you can get them. They will benefit everyone, especially children and the elderly.

Work less

If you must commute to work by car, can you change your work week of five eight-hour days to one of four ten-hour days? This can be a great solution, depending on the work you do and the cooperation of your employer. Can you telecommute at all, working one or two days a week from home and the rest at the office? Maybe, once you start decreasing your expenses, you'll find you can start to work part time. Maybe you can find a new job, something that is closer to home so that you can walk or ride your bike. Maybe you can find a new home closer to work. Maybe this is the time to start that home business or freelance career you've always wanted. See if you can save money by going in to work less.

Carpool to work, or use public transportation

It may be a little inconvenient to ride with colleagues to work, but it'll be so much better in the long run. You get to use the carpool lanes, and you don't always have to do the driving. If you can get your employer to offer incentives for carpooling, all the better. Many employers offer cash and a special place in the parking lot to carpoolers. Some employers offer mass-transit monthly pass cards. If your employer doesn't, see what you can do. It would serve them, and you, in the long run. Even if you have to pay for a pass yourself, it will be cheaper than driving, parking, fueling, insuring, repairing, registering, and replacing your car.

Don't forget to carpool with your friends for other activities like shopping, going to the beach or the movies, or attending religious services. You will cut down on expenses for both (or more) of you, and you'll have fun, too.

When it comes time for your vacation, consider what form of transportation is the most frugal. See Chapter Twelve: Travel for more ideas.

Drive a smaller car with higher gas mileage

Not only do larger vehicles use more fuel and belch out more carbon, they're more expensive to buy, insure, and maintain. If you have an SUV or other large vehicle, sell it and buy a smaller one. Choose a hybrid vehicle if you can afford it, or a small, high-mileage car with a regular engine. You may think you need the extra space found in a large vehicle, but you can fit quite a bit into even the smallest car. Don't be fooled into thinking that a large vehicle will protect you, either. Vigilant driving is the safest way to be on the road. Also, don't own a large vehicle just for the once or twice a year you need it to haul things; turn to a rental for those occasions, or borrow what you need from a friend.

Take care of your vehicle

A well-tuned and -maintained car with properly inflated tires will use less fuel and will last longer. After your home, the costs of owning a vehicle (or two) will take the next biggest chunk of your income. In that case, you'll want your vehicle (and please, only one!) to last as long as possible. Take care of it. The same goes for your bicycle: it needs regular tune-ups and maintenance also.

A car will last 200,000 miles or more. Don't even consider looking for a new car until your current vehicle can no longer be safely maintained.

Drive differently

Having owned a hybrid car with an ongoing computer readout of the current gas mileage, I can tell you that driving carefully raises your mileage significantly. Take secondary roads over high-speed freeways and interstates. Avoid fast starts and accelerations, and keep to the speed limit. It's hard to do when the traffic flow is five or ten miles per hour more than the speed limit, but it's safer, and you'll use less fuel. One friend says that keeping to the speed limit is a spiritual practice for him. Leave a few minutes early, and you won't feel the need to drive so fast.

Move closer to your work and/or closer to services

If you find you're spending a lot of time in the car simply because you live so far away from everything, you may want to consider moving (especially if you are already considering moving to a smaller house). Some people find they are able to live in a location that allows them to get rid of their vehicle altogether (or at least the second or third car). If you're committed to staying in your geographic area, explore the alternatives. A home near public transportation or a downtown shopping district or suburban mall may be worth the time and cost of moving — especially if you can drastically reduce your vehicle use (never mind your housing costs).

Get rid of your car and look into car-share (and bike-share) programs

You don't even have to own a car to use one for those times when walking or biking will not do. Many cities now have car-share programs where you arrange to use a vehicle now and then when you really need one. It's easier than renting, especially if you have need of a car on a periodic basis. You reserve the vehicle you want — they usually have cars, trucks, and vans to choose from — for the time you want and simply pay per trip. No hassles with rental companies, permanent parking, insurance, repairs, and replacement. Just sign up for what you need, when you need it, and leave the car care to others. Check out www.carsharing.net.

Some cities also have a similar programs with bicycles. Find out if yours does. Or consider co-owning a car with a friend or two.

Buy used

When it's time to look for a replacement vehicle, look for a used car, hybrid or regular. An older, conventional model may have excellent gas mileage, even approaching that of the new hybrids, so shop around and do your research. Since you no longer drive as much, or are as dependent on your car, owning a good used car is fine. Take care of it, and it will last for many years.

Not only does a new car lose a big chunk of its value as soon as you drive it out of the lot, car manufacturing is not the most environmentally friendly business on earth. A vast amount of planetary resources are used in building, and then trashing, all those vehicles we get around in. So buy used. You'll save money, and you'll help prevent all the associated environmental damage. It's the frugal thing to do.

9. Stuff

Ever since our ancestors created clothing from animal skins and tools from stone and bone, we have been inventing, crafting, purchasing, and collecting stuff. There's the stuff of basic living: clothing, cooking pots and utensils, containers to carry and store things, and furniture to sit and sleep on. Then there's all the other stuff: books, musical instruments, computers, power tools, lamps, toys, memorabilia, school supplies, briefcases, and sports equipment. Our stuff surrounds us, drives us to earn more money, creates clutter, brings comfort and happiness, and uses up resources of all kinds.

Our stuff is made of glass and plastic, cotton and wool, wood and metal, pottery and electronic components. These things are crafted by artisans, manufactured in overseas sweatshops, or built at American factories. All the material goods in our life have an origin in the earth and use resources when they are mined, smelted, tanned, woven, molded, screwed together, or transported. They all cost time and money, whether we purchase them new or used or get them for free.

In reality, we don't need much stuff to have a comfortable, fulfilled, and happy life. Think about how fun and easy it is to travel with only a backpack or a small bag. Recall the days when you were just starting out and you were thrilled to have your own place with cast-off furniture, a mattress on the floor, and rice and beans every night. Consider how babies and toddlers are easily entertained with some wooden spoons and saucepans as toys. Imagine that you are going to move abroad and can only take a limited amount of belongings, or that you have lost your home to fire or another disaster, and plan on replacing only those things that you truly love and need.

We need some stuff, certainly, but probably not everything that we currently own. There is great freedom in owning only those things you love and use on a regular basis. It's frugal to respect our possessions, be aware of them, and care for them, and to not bring into our lives any more things than necessary. Our stuff costs us, in the money it takes to purchase, fix, maintain, insure, store, and dispose of it as well as the time it takes to find it, clean it, care for it, put it away, and go looking for it again.

Here are some ways to help you become more frugal about your stuff.

Take an inventory of everything you own (and decide what you want to keep)

Yikes! Everything?

Yes, everything. This project will take you a while, so plan to do one room each weekend, or at a time when you have a couple of hours available and your energy level is good. If you have young children, they might like to help you. Make a game of it. If you do it by yourself, you can still make a game of it: wait until you're home alone, put on some music to get you going, get a cup of your favorite beverage and some sheets of scrap paper and a pen. Don't forget the attic, basement, garage, shed, and storage unit.

It is said that we use 20 percent of our stuff 80 percent of the time. Think about your own stuff and the 20/80 rule. I'll bet you have all kinds of clothes, jewelry, books, kitchen things, tools, and sporting equipment that you rarely, if ever, use. Keep this in mind as you go through your stuff.

You will be doing three things as you go through all your stuff: becoming aware of all you own, determining your net worth (see Chapter Thirteen: Money), and getting ready to get rid of all that you don't use, need, or love.

In preparation, along with your paper and pen, music and beverage, gather a good supply of boxes, a marker, and a trash bag. Working one room at a time, looking at absolutely everything, box up all the items you don't love, or that you have not used within the past year (this takes care of your seasonal items). Quality items go in a yard sale or donation box, broken but repairable items go in a to-be-fixed box, recyclable items in a recycling box, and the junk goes in a trash bag. Put aside files, documents, and memorabilia in another box to deal with later.

As you go through your books, jewelry, and clothes (often the hardest categories to sort), keep the "do you love it?" and "have you used it in the last year?" questions in mind. If it's a reference book and you haven't picked it up in the past year, ask yourself why you own it. If it's a novel that you loved and would read again, and it's unique enough that you don't think you'd find it at your local library, then by all means keep it. Otherwise, pack it away. The same goes for nonfiction, poetry, and other published works. If your children have outgrown their picture books or chapter books, ask them which ones they might like to save because they love them so much and might want to read again, and then box up the rest. If you cherish all your books, make sure they are shelved in a way that makes them accessible to you and attractive to see.

As for clothing and jewelry, if you haven't worn it in the past year, you probably won't wear it in the coming year either. If it is an expensive piece of clothing bought for a special occasion — a formal dress or suit, for example — ask yourself the following questions: Does it still fit? Would I ever go to another such formal event? Is the style timeless enough that I could wear it again? Do I really love it? If so, keep it. If not, put it in the yard-sale/give-away box. Look at the other clothes you don't wear, but are holding on to.

What's the point in keeping them? Sentimentality? Scarcity? Hoping to lose weight? Pack it away.

Use the same critical eye in every room, taking particular care with dishes and kitchen things, tools, sporting equipment, hobby supplies, and decorative items. Do you love it — really love it? Do you use it, or admire it, on a regular basis? If your house burned down, would you replace it immediately, or even try to rescue it from the flames? Forget the tools, skis, hobby supplies, games, and toys that are not used, even though you keep hoping that day will come. When and if you're really ready to take up that sport or hobby, you can always get the things you need, probably used and inexpensively or from someone else who doesn't use them.

One unexpected side effect of going through all your things is that you may discover items that were buried at the back of the closet, attic, or drawer that you do want and didn't realize you had. After you've sorted and boxed and can finally sit back and enjoy your stuff, you may feel like you have a whole new wardrobe, library, or kitchen without even spending a dime. It's also a delight to open a closet or cupboard and be able to put your hands on exactly what you're looking for without pawing through a bunch of unused stuff.

As you come across the ratty, junky, stained, and broken (and not reparable) things, have a heavy-duty trash bag at your side, and throw it away. If you wouldn't buy it at a yard sale, neither would anyone else. If it can be repaired, but you don't want to do it, offer it at the "free" corner of your yard sale or get a friend to fix it for you.

What about the rest of the people in your household? Can sorting be a group activity? It all depends on your family. Is everyone interested in doing this? Are all of you good at this kind of activity, or do some of you tend to get distracted or be unsure of your decisions? It may be best for the family member(s) who loves to do this to take the first pass through the all-family items. You can box up all the books you don't want, and then your partner or kids can go through the box to pick out things they do want without having to go through everything. The same can be done for other areas that tend to have many items, such as the workshop and the kitchen. Respect your family members who are different and who may struggle over this (especially yourself).

You can also assist your partner or children by going through their personal stuff, like clothes and toys, with them. Have a fashion show with your partner, and tell them which outfits you like on them and which you don't like. Tell your kids they can keep the money they earn by selling their stuff — that's a sure incentive to get them to sort with a critical eye. Help keep them going if need be; it's important to get a whole room done at once. Be gentle, though, and take your time with this project for everyone's sake. It can be very hard, emotionally and physically.

Once you are done going through a room and boxing and bagging up the stuff to get rid of, write down on your paper all that's left. Make this part easy on yourself by writing "200 paperbacks" or "10 wool sweaters," not listing each separate item (unless you really want to). When you have a room catalogued, assign a price to each item (what you would expect to pay for it at a yard sale or thrift shop, for example, not what it would cost new). Hold onto these papers for when you calculate your net worth.

Unless you're a very decisive, clear person, you may not be ready for a yard sale once you're done sorting. Label the boxes with the contents and the date, and store them in a clean, dry place. Once six months or a year goes by and you haven't looked for anything, then it's time to sell (or give away). In the meantime, you can enjoy the extra space that you have, the freed-up time in the morning spent looking through your wardrobe, and the joy in knowing that you won't have to rent that storage unit anymore or move to a larger home.

Have a big yard sale!

Now it's time for all those boxes and bags of stuff you no longer want or need to find a new home. Choose a popular yard-sale day or weekend, and get ready for a busy day. Don't forget to advertise your sale and have good signage. If you live in a poor location for a yard sale, consider holding yours with a friend who lives somewhere else, with an organization you're part of, or as a neighborhood-wide event. Visit other yard sales before your big day to check average prices and ways to display things. Have enough cash on hand to make change: people often arrive with tens or twenties. If you have kids, get them involved. They can help set things up, price, make signs, or staff their own table of electronics, toys and books.

If having a yard sale seems like more work than you want to take on, donate your items to your favorite charity. You can leave things with global charities such as the Salvation Army or Goodwill, or you can donate them to a local charity that holds an annual fundraising yard sale. They'll appreciate your things and will give you a letter stating the value of the items that you can use as a charitable tax deduction. If you do hold a yard sale, you can then donate any unsold items to charity. (Don't keep them! They'll only clutter up your newly uncluttered home.)

For larger, expensive items — sports equipment, appliances, small machinery, a car, etc. — you may want to advertise separately in your local paper or online, or just park them in your yard, price them, and see what happens. I once put a canoe in our yard with the asking price on it, sat on the front stoop reading, and talked to several interested buyers. The canoe was gone within the hour.

Once your stuff is gone, celebrate! Bank that money in your savings account and pat yourself and your helpers on the back for a job well done. Enjoy the extra space, the extra money, and the feel of an uncluttered house.

Use the library

Now it's time to make sure that clutter and excess stuff doesn't start to sneak back in. Books, as wonderful as they are, tend to multiply. Stop buying books (unless this is very important to you or you can work up a good trade system with your local used book store) and start using your local library. The same goes for recorded music and movies. Your library may have them, too.

As I've said before, libraries are wonderful. They are community institutions that offer much more than just books. They have magazines and newspapers, audio books, DVDs and videos, reference materials, computers, helpful staff, classes, and lectures. You could spend your whole life at the library and never begin to take advantage of everything that they have. Even if they don't have it, they can probably get it for you through interlibrary loan. Even if you don't live in a city, your small-town library (which may only be open once a week) still has more books than you could read in a lifetime, plus access to interlibrary loan.

If you read a book that you find you would like to own, for reference or pure pleasure in reading it over and over again, buy yourself a copy. Check for a used copy at your local used bookstore or online.

Keep an eye on your linens

One thing that we tend to have too much of is linens — towels, sheets, pillowcases, blankets, and other bed coverings. Often, we tire of what we have, and buy something new without considering whether or not the item we're using has outlived its useful life. Soon our linen closet is stuffed to the brim.

When you go through your linens, keep only those items you adore and that are still in good shape. No one really needs more than two sets of sheets and pillowcases, one to use and one to wash (and maybe a couple of flannel sets for those chilly nights). Hold on to just enough blankets or quilts for each member of the family to use at the coldest time of year, plus one or two for sleepovers and emergencies. As for towels, keep one set for each family member and a couple for guests and emergency messes.

Your excess linens can be used for a variety of purposes. Feel free to sell good-quality blankets at your yard sale, but consider donating the rest. The Red Cross or your local animal shelter is often happy to take old sheets, blankets, and towels. Save a few for rags (along with your old cotton T-shirts). If you, or someone you know, makes rag, hooked, or braided rugs or other fabric art, ask if they would like any of your things. Don't replace what you have until they are well worn and ready for the ragbag, and then be sure to purchase replacements on sale.

Beware of multiples of things

You may discover when you go through your things that you have excess multiples of some items. Nail clippers, scissors, and knives, in particular, tend to reproduce at alarming rates. How many do you actually need? Unless you have several chefs who like to chop vegetables at the same time, one or two chopping/paring knives for produce, cheese, and meats, and one serrated knife for breads and pastries is probably plenty. Get rid of those knives you don't really like, and have a whetstone to keep the ones you do use sharp. As for scissors, a general pair for kitchen use and cutting paper is all you need, unless you have someone in your household who sews, knits, or does other handcrafts that require special scissors. Look at all those other little things — nail files and clippers, tweezers, and the like — and see if you can reduce your numbers and take care of what you have. If you have just one, and it is stored in a designated place, chances are you'll find it when you need it.

Then there are the tools. Multiple screwdrivers, pliers, hammers, and other odds and ends are unnecessary, unless you're in the building trades or do woodworking as a hobby. Make yourself a toolbox or drawer that has one or two of each of the common household tools, and sell the rest at your yard sale. If you remember to put these items back in their box or drawer when you're done using them, you'll have no need to buy more.

Return items you don't really like

We're all human, and we all make impulse purchases. Perhaps we're rushed, or bored, or just want something new. Maybe we've ordered an item from a catalog or online, and, when it arrives, it's just not what we wanted. Or we have received a gift we don't really like or want.

Return it! Even if it costs you return postage or the time and gas to drive to the store (plan to do this with other errands), you'll save money in the long run. The unused or unworn item won't be taking up space in your closet or cupboard staring at you (and announcing "failure") every time you open the door. You'll have the purchase price, minus the cost of return, back in your pocket. You will then have the time to consider whether you want a replacement item that is right.

As for those unwanted gifts, if it's possible (relationship- and reality-wise) to return or exchange the item, do it. If you can't, maybe you have a friend that would like that tea set or scented candle. Otherwise, put unwanted gifts in a box destined for your next yard sale, donate them to charity, or save them to regift to others.

Be creative about storage

Anyone who has lived on a boat or in a recreational vehicle knows about limited storage and is also creative. Little cupboards in corners, under beds, or under chairs and couches are all used for storage. These places are often hard to get to and so are not used for items needed daily, but rather items needed periodically.

You can do the same thing in your home. There's no reason to pay good money to rent a storage unit. Perhaps once you have gone through all your things and eliminated what you don't want and don't love, you won't need that storage unit any more. But you still may have items that pose a storage challenge.

Some things can go under a bed or couch. Small, light-weight items can go on a high shelf in a closet (which you can install yourself). Consider hanging some things in a closet, pantry, or hallway. Don't start spending money on special storage containers when a cardboard box will do, or on special closet organizers when all you may need is to reorganize your stuff or put up another shelf.

You also don't have to store food in the kitchen, cleaning items under the sink, or extra toiletries and linens in the bathroom. If you've got a empty drawer in your bureau, it might be perfect for linens or small tools. If the closet in the bathroom has a couple of extra shelves, you can store canned goods or holiday decorations. Be willing to think creatively about your storage needs.

Go through your files

Now it's time to hit the file cabinet, desk drawer, or box stuffed in the back of the closet. Some household files are important — birth certificates, marriage license, divorce papers, wills, deeds, vehicle titles, investment documents. Organize them and keep them in a safe place. Home-organizing books have information about how long certain documents need to be kept. Hold onto tax records for seven years. Keep warranty and instruction information on the items you actually own and for which the warranty is still valid. Get rid of the ones for things you no longer have. If you plan to sell or give away some of these things, store the information with the item for use by the new owner.

Once you've sorted out the legal documents, instruction manuals, and warranty papers, you'll probably find that other files belong in the "memorabilia" category. Put these special things aside for organizing later (see below). Other miscellaneous files of information generally don't need to be kept unless you actually refer to them periodically, so recycle them. If you find you need the information later, you can probably find it at the library or on the Internet. When you recycle the papers you don't want anymore, be careful to burn or shred any documents with Social Security numbers or other sensitive information.

By the time you're done, you may discover you no longer need your file cabinet, and that all your documents easily fit into a small box or bag. Your house just got a little bigger.

Care for your memorabilia and family heirlooms

We all have photos, newspaper clippings, greeting cards, letters, and other things that are important to us. For many of us, that stuff is just tossed in a box or in a desk drawer to be dealt with later. Well, later has come. Our memorabilia, if it is truly important to us, should be stored so that we can look at it and enjoy it, as well as in a way that preserves it for posterity.

When you went through all your stuff, you put your memorabilia and heirlooms in a box and set it aside for later sorting and organizing. This can be a very emotional experience, so be prepared. First you sort, and then you determine just what kind of storage equipment you actually need. Give yourself an uninterrupted time to do this.

As you sort, ask yourself if the item will hold up to the passage of time, and if it would be important to refer to again or to leave for your descendents. If you've saved all your — and your children's — report cards, ask yourself why. If you've saved every drawing and painting your child has ever produced, choose one or two favorites from each year. If you have hundreds of photos of your firstborn, and only a handful of the rest of the kids, even it out. Get rid of things that no longer hold meaning or that you have no idea when and where they're from. To save space (and keep up with new technology), you can have DVDs made of old slides or home videos that will excerpt the most important scenes and events.

When you have assembled everything you want to keep, get yourself a photo album or scrapbook. Sort your items by the category of your choice — year, child, trip, event — and put them in the book. Be sure to label everything: there's nothing worse than an old yellowed photo of a family reunion of people nobody knows. If you're saving this stuff for future generations, make sure they understand the importance of it — otherwise, don't keep it.

For items that can't go into scrapbooks or photo albums, get a sturdy, waterproof, fireproof box. Make sure you store this box in a cool, dry, dark place. Get into the habit of putting new items away in the scrapbook or memorabilia box as soon as possible after the event, while your memory is fresh, so that the boxes of clutter don't start to build up again. You can put older children in charge of their own scrapbooks and photo albums.

As for family heirlooms — Grandmother's silver or china, Grandfather's pocket watch, Aunt Mary's engagement ring, Uncle Fred's collection of elephant statues — first decide if you really want to keep them. If they don't hold meaning for you, someone else in your family may want them. If no one else wants them, you can sell them through an antiques dealer or on the Internet. Computer technology also allows us to take photos of these items, if you want to remember them without owning them — maybe Uncle Fred's elephants would look better as your desktop photo.

If you do keep them, then use them! Put your mismatched dishes in your yard sale and eat from — and enjoy — your grandmother's china. Wear the jewelry, have a special shelf for the elephant statues, and use the silver. Get pleasure from these special items, and respect your ancestors for the lives they led. These things from a long time ago are often of better quality than those that are made today. Think about which of your belongings will be considered precious by your descendants.

Create a toy exchange

Once your children sort through their toys and keep what they love and use, they will eventually tire of what they have (or outgrow it) and want new things. Other people's children will do the same. Start a toy exchange!

Get your friends, neighbors, and colleagues together to pool the toys their children, grandchildren, nieces, and nephews no longer want or use. Find a space in someone's home, at your workplace, at your church or synagogue, or at your public library to house the collection of toys, games, puzzles, musical instruments, and sports equipment. Create your own rules for taking and adding things. Items should be clean and complete (no missing game and puzzle pieces, for example), and sorted by age or activity.

Perhaps users of the exchange need to bring in an item to get a new item. It's up to you.

Get together with other parents, grandparents, aunts, and uncles to set this up. Everyone will be grateful for this frugal and community-minded service and will be thrilled to have unused toys out of the house and into the hands of someone who will enjoy them.

Take care of your things

So, now what's left is what you love and what you use. Take care of your belongings. Oil your sewing machine. Have your shoes and boots resoled. Keep tools and toys out of the rain. Wash, repair, polish, vacuum, and store in an appropriate place all that you own. Our things are precious — it is an honor to be able to own them. If you don't believe that, take a look at an amazing book called *Material World* (Peter Menzel, Sierra Club Books, 1994). This book chronicles the homes and belongings of people from various places all over the world. When you look at the pictures and read about the family in Mali with only a few baskets and blankets, some utensils, a goat, and a bike, or the family in Mongolia with a yurt, some rugs, and a few cooking pots, you will know your things are special.

If you don't know how to do simple home repairs, then learn. Ask a friend or the folks at the hardware store to teach you, or take a class. Clothes can be mended, appliances and furniture repaired, skis tuned, and oil changed. If you are all thumbs, see if you can trade another service with a friend who is handy. Perhaps you can watch their toddler or walk their dog if they rewire your lamp or change your oil.

Put things away when you're done with them. Keep your scissors and knives sharpened, your knitting needles or sewing accessories in one place, your tools oiled, your house painted, and your leather goods protected with saddle soap. With fewer things that you use more often, this will be easier — and more important — to do.

Remember the "one thing in, one thing out" rule

Now that all that clutter and excess is out of the house, don't let it back in. It is so easy to have slow-stuff-creep. People give you gifts, you pick up some new bowls on sale, you find yourself wanting a new piece of clothing or a book. If you really want and need that new item, fine, but try to follow the "one thing in, one thing out" rule to stay in balance.

You've bought new bowls? Then put the old ones in a box labeled for the next yard sale. Take up shopping at your local used-clothing consignment shop and trade in old but still good clothes for new-to-you ones. Encourage your friends and relatives to cut back on gifts, but if you do receive something beautiful and wonderful, be thankful and enjoy it. Just look around your house and see what you have that you no longer want or need, and tuck it into the yard-sale box in exchange for your lovely gift. (Gifts that you don't want can be returned to the store, passed on to someone else, or immediately put in the yard-sale box.)

If something breaks, wait a while to replace it to see

if you really need it. Often you can find another way to do the same thing. The wineglasses are all gone? Drink out of a mug or tumbler. The calculator died? Use the one on your computer, or go back to doing math by hand. A recipe calls for an eight-by-eight baking dish and you don't have one? Use that nine-inch cast-iron frying pan instead. There are often several different ways to accomplish what you want. Be creative.

Ask yourself before you make any purchase, Do I really need this? Can I get the same thing in another way? Does this purchase fit my values and my life? Beware the latest fad, be it electronics, hobby supplies, toys, fashion, or vehicles.

When you buy, plan ahead to buy used, buy locally, and buy quality

For those items you do need to buy, first see if you can find them used. Clothes, books, sporting equipment, vehicles, bikes, and large tools are easily found at thrift shops, in the "for sale" section of your local paper, or online. Yard sales or "junk" stores are good for kitchen things, games, jigsaw puzzles, small tools, paint, furniture, and books. You may remember that a friend has what you want and doesn't use it. Offer to buy it or barter for it. Get your friends together for a clothing swap, a book swap, or a toy swap. Get your neighbors together to form a tool cooperative — why does every family need their own lawnmower, circular saw, shovel, or wheelbarrow, when these items are not used every day?

If you need something brand new — office supplies, hardware, underwear, and the like — shop at a locally owned store, not a major chain or big box store. You may pay a bit more, but you are investing in your community. It's well worth it. Not only will you be avoiding the aggravation of the traffic, parking, and crowd problems at the big stores (and the gas you'll use to get there), you'll be supporting your downtown merchants (who are probably your neighbors) and helping to reduce the sprawl that is destroying our precious green space.

While you're buying that new item, consider quality over price — it may be the more frugal thing to do. A three-hundred-dollar sewing machine that will last twenty years or more is a much better investment than a hundred-dollar machine that will give out after five years. Better to spend the money now for a quality item that will give you many more years of hassle-free service than to buy one that is cheap in every sense of the word.

Make sure you plan ahead when buying anything. If you can anticipate your needs, you can shop around for a used item, keep an eye out for sales, or find out if you can co-own it with a friend or neighbor. Many items are on sale at certain times of year (linens in January, for example), and many communities have winter sports equipment swaps in the fall and bike swaps in the spring. Learn what's going on in your area. By taking the time to find just what you want at the best price, you'll save yourself a lot in the long term — and, possibly, you may decide that you don't need the item after all.

Use it up, wear it out, make do, or do without

Above all, follow this old adage. We really don't need that much stuff, and what we have should bring us pleasure to use and care for. Remember those people around the world who have very little. Respect what you do have and take care of it. Think twice before buying something brand new or new to you. So often we shop mindlessly, whether at a yard sale or at the mall. We are drawn to bargains ("the more you spend, the more you save!"), but acquiring new things we don't really need is no bargain at all, whatever the price. Not taking care of our stuff is akin to not taking care of our bodies. Owning less stuff, taking care of and enjoying what we do have, and being thoughtful about future purchases can bring us a great feeling of freedom — and cash in the bank.

10. Health and body

Our bodies are precious and allow us to enjoy our lives to the fullest. Like many things, however, they break down from time to time. Our habits, our emotions, our work, our play, and our environment all contribute to our health, or lack thereof. Our access to quality health care also contributes to our quality of life. Many, many people in our world — including the United States — do not have access to safe, affordable health care. Even those who do have access to doctors and hospitals may find they cannot afford copays and pharmaceuticals.

We need to learn to take care of ourselves, in sickness and in health. We need to learn how to enjoy and appreciate our bodies for what they can, and cannot, do and be. Not everyone will be an Olympic athlete or a supermodel. Not everyone will be slender or tall. Acceptance of our gifts and limitations will go a long way toward improving our health and well-being.

It doesn't have to cost us a fortune in time and money to care for our bodies over their lifespan. Whether it's how we choose to style our hair, take care of ourselves when we don't feel well, or use our muscles, there are many ways to achieve the same goals. By learning to understand your body and its particular needs and quirks, you will find freedom from the many pundits who love to tell you how you should look and feel. Your body is yours: you don't have to go into debt to feel — and be — beautiful and healthy.

There are many frugal things you can do to enhance and care for your body from birth to death. Here are some ideas.

Take care of your body

If you take care of yourself, you'll need fewer medications and trips to the doctor. Everyone knows that good food, regular exercise, plenty of sleep, and daily brushing and flossing are all ways to keep our bodies in good shape. Find ways to incorporate these good habits into your life.

Learn how your body works. If you have children in your life, this is a great activity to do with them. Get some library books about the human body, or look in an encyclopedia or online. Play games with the information you learn (some books even suggest games and activities). The more you know about your body and how its "machinery" works, the less those little aches and pains and tummy upsets will send you to the doctor. You will understand where they come from, how to relieve the symptoms, and how to prevent them from happening so often.

Despite the metaphor of our body as machine, it's also important to understand that many other factors affect how we feel, not just a broken cog easily repaired. Our stress levels, our relationships, our emotions, and our worries affect our health and can eventually take a toll on our bodies. We need to listen to those little voices that tell us not to eat certain foods, not to have certain conversations with certain people, or not to keep at it when it's clear we need to take a break and rest.

Pay attention to safety as well. Many injuries happen when we do something foolish. Learn to use your body properly when lifting heavy objects or moving furniture, make sure ladders are secure before climbing them, see that your area rugs stay in place, drive defensively with a seat belt and within the speed limit, and use helmets and other safety gear when participating in certain sports.

Learn to love your body. We come in different shapes and sizes, and while everyone needs exercise and nutritious food, we will not all be the same weight, height, and strength no matter how hard we diet or work out. Accept your unique appearance and take care of yourself. Find some sort of way to use your body that brings you joy, and eat your plant-based, seasonal meals with equal relish.

Stop your bad habits

There are many tempting things to eat, drink, and do that are not so good for our bodies — or our wallets.

Smoking, taking recreational drugs, using alcohol and caffeine to excess, gambling, driving at excessive speeds, and having unprotected sex with multiple partners are all bad habits that are damaging to us in many ways. Consider the things you do that could not only save you a lot of money if you stopped doing them, but could also save your life.

Learn when to call or see the doctor

Everyone becomes ill at one time or another. Often it is as simple as a cold, a headache, or an upset stomach. Other times we injure ourselves — a sprained ankle, a broken bone, or a wound in need of stitches and a tetanus shot. On other occasions, it seems that something is seriously wrong with our bodies.

Talk to your doctor about the appropriate time to call him or her. Simple things that tend to go away over a short period of time generally do not need to be cared for by a doctor or even a nurse. Bedrest and fluids for a cold, a nap and some pain reliever for a headache, mint tea and the passage of time for an upset stomach — use common sense when it comes to short-lived aches and pains.

Your doctor will want to talk to you, or see you, if your fever is at or above a certain point, if that nagging cough has lingered more than a few weeks, or if your swollen ankle hasn't improved in a few days. Every doctor has different criteria, so ask. At the same time, ask your doctor for information about how to care for simple illnesses and injuries in the home. Basic knowledge about care for common complaints has fallen by the wayside. Take the time to learn.

In addition to visits to your health-care provider when you're ill or in pain, many doctors want to see you for an annual checkup or specific "preventative" tests, immunizations, and the like. Ask your doctor why you need these (potentially expensive) tests and checkups, and don't immediately take his or her word for it. Do your own research, ask questions, and learn to say no. Our health-care system takes up an extraordinary amount of our personal, financial, and societal resources. Think twice before you spend yours.

Clean out your medicine chest

The average medicine chest is full of over-the-counter (OTC) remedies for everything from heartburn, stuffy noses, and coughs to seasonal allergies, diarrhea, and constipation, along with current and past-date unused prescription drugs. As you learn how to take care of minor injuries and illnesses at home without medications, you can throw the lot out except for the one OTC pain medication you prefer (aspirin, acetaminophen, or ibuprofen), plus your current prescriptions. Be sure to get rid of any outdated or partially used prescriptions and OTC remedies in a safe manner.

Toss any other old, dried-up products that are taking up space. Plan to keep some basic first-aid supplies: adhesive bandages, hydrogen peroxide, gauze pads and tape, and that bottle of your preferred pain medication. If you should need a prescription medication, be sure to follow the directions and use it up. (If you take a prescription medication on a regular basis, talk with your doctor about what you could do to get off the medication and whether or not you can get a cheaper, generic version. In the meantime, be sure to take as directed and store in a safe place.)

While you're at it, go through all the other items on your bathroom shelves: travel shampoos, gift soaps, old razors, empty bottles, and what-have-you. Plan to use up all the various shampoos, lotions, etc. before you buy any more. If you don't like the unused products taking up space on your shelves, donate them to your local homeless or battered-women's shelter. Think twice before you buy any new personal-care products. Do you still have some at home? Do you really need it? Is there another way to accomplish the same task? Many personal-care items and herbal medicines can be made at home from simple ingredients. If this interests you, there are many good books on the subject; check your local library.

Learn simple home remedies

Our grandmothers, and maybe even our mothers, knew how to handle the minor complaints of the body. They knew to make chicken soup for a cold, weak tea and toast for a recovering upset stomach, rice and applesauce for diarrhea. They knew that rest was important for most injuries and illnesses. They knew about putting ice on an injury at first and heat later on. They knew to elevate sprains, and how to create a sling to hold an injured arm.

You can learn about common and simple-to-make home remedies from any number of books on the subject. Herbal teas are easy to make, and herbal tinctures are not much harder. Many medicinal herbs grow wild where you live and are easy to identify. Basic home-care herbs like mint, catnip, chamomile, dandelion, motherwort, and nettle have few, if any, side effects and are safe to use for the whole family.

Learn some basic first aid as well: what to do in case of minor — and major — injuries. Your local Red Cross or community hospital may offer classes. Everyone should know CPR, the Heimlich maneuver, how to care for someone in shock, and how to care for simple wounds and injuries. You never know when you may be the first on the scene of an accident, one that may even be in your own home. Your knowledge could save someone's life or soothe the spirit of a child in the wee hours of the morning.

Stop taking supplements and over-the-counter drugs

Many people take vitamins and minerals, protein powders, and other various supplements on a regular basis. Consider why you take supplements. Are you not taking the time to eat properly? Are you stressed out, always in a hurry? Do you have frequent stomach upsets, joint aches, or headaches that have led you to take supplements or over-the-counter remedies of some kind?

Look at why you might have that ongoing headache, stomachache, or backache. Is it a food that's not agreeing with you? Are you allergic to dusts and molds, yet don't clean your house on a regular basis? Do you drink too much coffee or alcohol? Not enough water? Are you constipated? Try drinking more water, eating more fruits and vegetables, and taking the time to use the toilet. Can't fall asleep? Cut back on caffeine, ditch the sleeping pills, and try some catnip tea and relaxation exercises. Many of our common aches, pains, and physical annoyances have their origin in some imbalance in our lives. We're all different, so you'll have to do some investigative work to uncover yours. You'll feel better in the long run if you make some adjustments in your habits or your lifestyle, and you'll save money when you don't need all those supplements and OTC medications.

Give up your health-club membership, and find a no-cost/low-cost way to exercise

If you're starting to walk more while you do errands, or you've started to commute to work without using a car, you'll automatically be getting regular exercise. Combine that with biking — for commuting, errands, visiting friends, or simply for fun — and that's even more exercise. You're hanging up the laundry, doing your own cooking, clearing the snow by hand, and tending a small garden. Congratulations: you're getting in shape.

Now, why is it that you still have that gym membership? Into weight training? Try stacking wood, carrying toddlers, or lifting encyclopedias. Love using the pool? Treat yourself to a day pass if you feel like swimming, or find a free public beach you can use. Like to play racquet-ball with your friends? If this is a priority, and you really love the sport, go ahead. Otherwise, consider taking up tennis and using the public tennis courts, or try tossing a Frisbee around with your friends.

As with everything else, think about why you have a health-club membership, and see if you can achieve the same purpose without spending the money. Exercise is important, but there are many ways to strengthen our muscles, lungs, and hearts without paying through the nose. A daily half-hour walk is all you really need. Besides strengthening and toning your body, walking can be relaxing and fun. Give it a try.

Stop wearing makeup

If you feel you can't leave home without lipstick or nail polish, think about why that is. Many people say they feel undressed. Some think that makeup is required for certain professions in our society. Others feel that they look better with makeup, but in my experience that doesn't hold true. How would you feel if you left home without makeup?

There are myriad reasons for not wearing makeup. Besides the expense, there is the time it takes to apply it and fix it throughout the day, the chemicals used in the products, and the animal testing done by some cosmetic companies. There are all the plastic and metal containers that have to be manufactured and then thrown away. There's all the space that you need to store your items, and the time it takes to shop for new products.

Some people like to wear makeup for fun on a special occasion. If that's you, then pick a product or two that you love that is manufactured in a safe way without animal testing, and have a good time! Otherwise, throw it all out and free yourself from the tyranny and the cost of makeup.

Get a no-fuss hairstyle

The same goes for your hair. How many products, and how much time, does it take to get your hair ready in the morning? As with makeup, many people think they need styled hair to function in our society, especially at certain occasions and at certain jobs.

Think about your hair. What do you like, and not like, about your hair and your current hairstyle? Can you imagine another way to wear your hair that would require less work and fewer products? Do you color or perm your hair? Why? Is this something you could do without? Your hairdresser will have some ideas about a simpler hairstyle that is flattering to you, although you may meet some resistance: hairdressers like to sell their products and their services. If that's your case, find a new hairdresser (or no hairdresser at all).

A simpler hairstyle will mean no blow dryer, gel, or mousse. It will probably mean less shampoo and washing time. It will mean less preparation time, and fewer trips to get it cut. If you have a very simple hairstyle and a friend or family member with skills in this area, you can trade haircuts for another service.

All in all, a simpler hairstyle will save you time and money. Besides, bad hair days will happen anyway, no matter your style.

Look at health-insurance alternatives

If you and your family are paying too much for health insurance, look at the alternatives. Everyone's health is different, every state has different companies that have different kinds of policies, and some states have their own health-insurance plans for people with low or low-moderate income. You can get full coverage, partial coverage, catastrophic coverage, coverage only for your children, or no coverage at all.

Our country has reached a crisis in health care that has been building over many years. Congress periodically tackles this issue, but has not yet found an equitable solution; health-insurance companies, drug companies, and physicians all have powerful lobbies. Even if you do have insurance, you may not be covered for certain illnesses, surgeries, procedures, or tests. Think about how you use the health-care system. Is it possible to go without insurance (or have only catastrophic insurance) if you and your family have no chronic illnesses and feel comfortable caring for minor illnesses and injuries at home?

Hospitals are required to provide a certain amount of free and reduced-cost care. There are many clinics and other organizations that provide low-cost or donation-only care. Look into what is available in your area. Doctors and hospitals radically mark up every visit and procedure to cover all their expenses, malpractice insurance, the people who need free care, and the cost of medical school. You can often bargain with a doctor or hospital for a reduced rate that may be more in line with actual costs, and some health-care providers may even be willing to barter with you. It doesn't hurt to ask.

A national health-care system would be best for everyone, so we should all be lobbying our elected officials about this important issue. Many, many citizens are without any health insurance at all, and, at the same time, many people are abusing the system, going to the doctor for every little complaint when most illnesses would go away with time and some simple, common-sense home remedies. Many people without insurance have learned to get health care on a pay-as-you-go basis. It's up to you to decide what is best for you and your loved ones. Consider how you consume health-care resources. Is there any way to pay less and use less?

Care for your ill or aging family members at home

One hundred years ago almost everyone was cared for at home. Doctors routinely made house calls, and hospitalizations were saved for the most severe cases. Our grandparents lived at home until they died, cared for by their children, grandchildren, and great-grandchildren. Babies were born at home, and someone with broken bones — once they were set — healed in their own bed.

Caring for our sick and dying loved ones is a lost art. It is not difficult, physically; the challenge is usually emotional, as the needs of the ill, injured, or aged are many. We don't want our regular lives, our time at work, or our leisure time with friends to be interrupted. But there is no greater gift you can give to your loved ones than caring for them when they need care. You'd probably want them to do the same for you.

The cost of extended hospital stays and nursing home care is enormous, both to us personally and to our society. Many people at the end of life use far too many medical resources in an attempt to stay alive a few more minutes, hours, or days. The end of life and the aging process can be messy and uncomfortable, but it is part of who we are. Consider what you would want at the end of your life.

If you decide you want to care for your loved ones at home, you don't have to do it in isolation. Hospice and home-care nurses, nurses' aides, and other health-care professionals are available to assist you. (Some services are covered by insurance; others need to be paid for out of pocket.) Support groups, in person or online, abound. Enlist the support of other family members and friends, or people from your religious community. If everyone takes turns cooking, doing laundry, cleaning the house, taking someone out for a ride, running errands, or sitting at someone's bedside, then the burden will be lessened for everyone.

Talk about this with your loved ones. Learn some practical skills: how to give a bed bath or change the sheets while someone remains in bed, for example. Think about how your home could be rearranged to accommodate an ill or dying person. Be honest about your limitations — and your know-how. The freedom we gain through living frugally is not just a selfish freedom, but also a freedom that allows us to spend time with others. Caring for our loved ones at home will save money, yes, and it will also provide everyone with a rich experience.

Write your will and durable power of attorney for health care

Every adult should have a completed last will and testament and a power of attorney for health care/living will. It's the best, final gift you can give your loved ones. If you should die suddenly or be incapacitated, your family's grief will be lessened if you have left clear instructions about your desires for your care and the disposal of your body and your property. There will be less emotional and financial cost to your family if you prepare these documents ahead of time. Whether you have just a few assets, or many, it's not hard to complete these documents yourself.

There are many books on the subject, and boilerplate documents are available online, in books, and at your local hospital or doctor's office. You simply need to fill them out and have them witnessed by your state's required number of people. Be sure to give copies of your living will to your doctor, hospital, and the person who will be responsible for decision-making on your behalf, and carry one in your wallet, purse, or glove compartment.

As for your last will and testament, once that is written, signed, and appropriately witnessed, keep it in a safe place, and give a copy to your next of kin. Don't forget to talk about the contents of both documents with loved ones and include instructions for what you would like done after death with your body and for your memorial service or funeral. These are hard conversations to have, but so important. I have stood by too many family members who struggled to make these decisions without any idea of what their loved one would have wanted. Enlist the support of a friend or clergy person if you need help with this process.

11. Fun

For many of us, what we do in our spare time is more important than what we do for work. We love to play — whether at sports, on a musical instrument, with a deck of cards, or by creating art, going to the theater, or attending a concert. We travel to exotic and foreign locales (or wish we could), sometimes planning for years to have the trip of our dreams.

Doing fun things is good for our souls, our bodies, our minds, and our spirits. We get to spend time with family and friends in a more relaxed way. Having fun is great — or is it?

Unfortunately, many people feel they have to spend money — large and small amounts — to have a good time. Some people continually try out new and popular hobbies (collecting unused equipment and supplies in the meantime) or wish they could. Others think that they must go on a big vacation every year, even if it puts them in debt and causes family strife. Others have a great pastime but still seem to spend too much money buying the latest gear and gizmos for their avocation.

The key is to find out what activities you really love and focus on those. Sure, you'll spend some money in the quest for pleasure, but you don't have to break the bank. There are many ways to get what you want without spending a lot of time, money, and stress just to have "fun." Make sure that how you choose to play is truly playful, for you and those around you.

Here are some ways that you can have frugal fun.

Consider how and why you use paid entertainment

Think of what you spend money on in the name of "having fun." This can be anything from shopping to going to the movies to taking the kids to an amusement park. It can be renting videos or watching cable TV. It can be attending plays or concerts, or going to a pool, waterfront, or recreation area that has an admission fee. Look at all the ways you spend money to have fun.

Does this bring you fulfillment? Do you absolutely love one, or more, of the activities you pay for? Is it worth the time and money you put into it? Could you find the same fun and fulfillment without paying for it, in cash and in the time it takes to earn that cash?

For example, if you love attending the theater, you can

often attend a play for no or low cost by volunteering to be an usher, doing some other work for the organization, or purchasing reduced-price tickets at the last minute at the box office or through another venue. Just ask your favorite community or professional theater company what you can do for them. As an added benefit, you'll get to meet the actors and production staff and learn more about the back-stage work of the theater.

On the other hand, if you buy entertainment because you are bored, or need to relax, or feel the kids deserve some fun on Saturday afternoon, think of other ways you can relieve boredom, relax, or have fun. If you're bored, find an activity that you love to do that brings you good energy and a sense of pride and fulfillment. If you want to relax, you can read, take a walk or a nap, have a bath, do crossword puzzles, play a musical instrument, or talk with a friend. If you want to have fun with your kids (or your friends!), they might love an afternoon of Monopoly or Trivial Pursuit or playing with Legos — with you — rather than going to an amusement park. Remember, you are teaching them values with your actions. If you constantly pay for them to be entertained, they will seek the same things when they grow up. There is no greater gift we can give to our children, or to ourselves and our friends, than the gift of time and attention.

Consider how and why you use vacation time

Are you fond of vacating your life on a regular basis? Do you look forward to a week in a tropical place, at a ski area, on a lake, or in a nice hotel in a new city? Does the time off mean a great deal to you, or are you constantly checking e-mail and cellphone messages, fussing about work, and waiting to get back? Do you worry that you can't afford a nice vacation? Do you even get paid time off?

Vacations mean different things to different people: a chance to not work, a chance to visit friends and family, a chance to stay home, a chance to travel, a chance to sleep late. What does it mean to you? Is your time off from paid work enhancing your life or putting you deeper into debt? Is it causing more stress or bringing joy to your heart?

Consider what you would do with your time if you were no longer working forty-plus hours a week. Would you still want to take a week, or two or three, a year to visit family and friends, travel to an exotic location, or go to a family-centered amusement park or other facility? Would you want to spend more time doing these things, or less?

Most everyone loves to travel. Most everyone loves to visit old friends. Most everyone likes to see new sights. But these things are different from vacating. Vacations simply give you time away from your paid work, generally while still being paid. It's your life. How do you want to spend your time?

Perhaps vacation time is the one time in a year when your whole family can be together. That alone is very special. Does it become more special, or more stressful, to go on a long trip to a foreign country, a national park, or Cousin Betty's house? Maybe it would be more fun to stay home and take in the sights that tourists come to your area to see. Maybe it would be more fun to have a picnic in the park every day, play badminton, and read books. Maybe it would be more fun to just hang out and see what happens. Think about it.

For more thoughts on frugal vacations and travel, see chapter twelve.

Consider how you spend your time away from work

What do you love to do when you're not at work? What do you actually do when you're not at work?

Many of us have hobbies that we enjoy. Crafts are popular: knitting, quilting, woodworking, basket making, weaving, pottery, and such. Other artistic endeavors rate right up there, too: making music, painting, sculpting, writing poetry. Other people love to use their bodies for fun: swimming, boating, biking, hiking, skating, skiing, rock climbing. Still others find joy in quieter pastimes such as cooking, winemaking, reading, or gardening.

Do you have something that you spend time doing that brings you personal fulfillment, that expresses your creativity, that you can't wait to do when you have the time? Or do you have a bunch of hobby-projects stacked up in the corner of the basement just waiting for all that free time you'll have one day? Do you tend to try every new fad hobby that comes along? Or are you at a loss for something creative and meaningful to do?

What happens in your home during evenings, weekends, or time off? Do you do household chores, veg out in front of the TV or computer screen, play games with your family, bug your kids about their homework and their friends, find time for your partner, visit friends, sleep? When it's time to go back to work after some time off, do you look back on that free time with happiness or disgust?

Think about what you love to do — or might love to do — and do it. But don't run right out and sign up for classes and purchase all kinds of supplies. Start slowly and start small. If you want to write, grab a pen and some paper and just write about what you see out your window. The novel will come later. If you want to draw, get a pencil and paper and start by sketching what's in your house or at a nearby park. The oils and canvas will come in time. If you want to knit, make a hat or a pair of mittens before you tackle a complicated sweater. Start now and discover what you love to do.

Get rid of your TV

Watching television seems to be the major way that people entertain themselves today, though using the computer probably comes in a close second. Besides the amount of money you spend on purchasing a television and subscribing to cable or satellite services, your TV may also use a lot of electricity, depending on its size and quality. The time you spend watching television drains you of financial resources and, often, drains you of physical and mental energy that would be better spent doing something more fulfilling.

Consider why you watch television. Is it because you don't know what else to do? Is it because you want to keep up on the latest news? Is it because you have certain programs that you like, with characters and plot that interest you? Is it because you love sports and want to follow your favorite teams? Is it because you love watching movies? If you find you're watching TV for no good reason at all, try going without for a week. You can choose TV Turn Off week (usually at the end of April) if you want support from others, or you can just pick any time that works for you. If you don't consider yourself an addict but generally sit down to one or more favorite sitcoms or dramas, try recording them (if you have the capability) and wait until the end of the month to watch several shows in a row. If you watch the news regularly, try getting your news from other sources such as the radio or the Internet, or take a news vacation: do without any news for several days, weeks, or months. If you watch TV for sports, try listening to the game on the radio, watching with a friend, or going a local bar (the cost of one beer per game will be far less than your electricity and cable bill). If you have a TV just to watch movies, use your computer instead. Experiment with different ways of getting what you want and with not watching television at all.

This is a good time to cancel your cable subscription as well. Fewer channels to choose from will mean fewer shows to watch. Think of the money for fees and electricity that you'll save, never mind the time you'll gain. Use the extra time to pursue that hobby that you've discovered or to spend time with your family and friends.

Perhaps you'll be ready to stop watching TV altogether. Sell all your equipment (do you have a TV in every room?) at your next yard sale and enjoy the extra space, the extra time, and the extra money.

Consider your computer usage

Just as with television, using a computer can become addictive. How much time do you spend playing computer games, surfing the Internet, watching stuff on YouTube, and checking up on your friends on Facebook? Are these activities making your life more fulfilling, or are they simply a way to pass the time? Only you can decide.

Try limiting your computer time to an hour (or less) per day, or just take a break altogether for a day, a week, or a month. See how it feels to go without and how it feels to have time to do something else. Experiment. Your computer usage costs you mentally, as well as financially for the cost of the equipment (updated frequently), the Internet service, and the electricity. Perhaps you might even consider selling your computer and using one at the library when you need to check e-mail or search for something online.

Learn to play cards and board games

You don't have to play Scrabble and solitaire on the computer: these games can be played with real tiles and real cards. So can poker, pinochle, bridge, Trivial Pursuit, and Parcheesi. You may have fond (and not-so-fond) memories of playing games when you were a kid. You can still play them — and this time, you don't have to play with your mean older brother who always beat you.

People of any age love cards and board games. A wide variety of games are available today for very young children, so you don't have to play Candy Land and crazy eights if you don't want to. The older set still loves Monopoly, Scrabble, Cranium, Pictionary, and Trivial Pursuit. Adults tend to focus on bridge and poker, but can enjoy any of the games that older children like. New games are being invented all the time, and games — old or new — are a great way to use our minds and have fun with our friends and family.

Visit a good toy store to see what's available. Ask the sales clerks for recommendations based on your interests and the age of the players. Some people prefer math-oriented games, while others like trivia or word games. Some like games with partners; others like to be on their own. Sometimes your library may offer a game day, where you can go and try out new games you may not be familiar with. Be sure to take the kids — and the grandparents.

Once you've found a game or two you'd like to try, see if you can buy it at a yard sale, try it out at the library, or borrow it from a friend before you buy it new. If you really love a game, it may make sense to buy new and take care of it. We're on our fourth or fifth set of Five Crowns cards, a great game for almost any age. Every dollar we spent on those cards has been well worth it for the hours and hours of fun we've had. You can also set up a game exchange with other people who love to play games.

Learn to enjoy silence and solitude

As the information highway has gotten more complicated, and electronic-entertainment technology has advanced, we spend less and less time alone and in silence. If we happen to be home by ourselves, we turn on the TV or radio for company. We get nervous in the stillness and seek companionship — or distraction.

Try stopping yourself from using electronic media as your friend, and try spending time without that background noise. Take a walk, or sit in a comfortable chair and look out the window. Read. Write in a journal. Sing. Practice your craft, your art, or your musical instrument. Learn to enjoy your own company and that of the natural world. It can be more relaxing than the constant buzz that comes from electronics, and it is absolutely free.

Find frugal ways to be with friends

How often do you get together with friends over a restaurant meal, dancing at a club, or at a movie, play, or concert? Are your friendships costing you more money than you'd like? Find different ways to spend time with your best buddies.

You can organize a potluck or a progressive meal (appetizers at one house, dinner at the next, dessert somewhere else). You can suggest going out for drinks or dessert and forgo the expensive meal. You can play cards or board games, go for a hike, ride bikes, get together to play music, or read aloud a play (be sure to assign roles in advance so people can practice!). Or you can simply chat over tea in someone's living room.

Whether it's by yourself, with family, or with friends, learn to have fun without spending any money. It's easy to do: just be creative. Your friends might appreciate the money they'll save as well. It's the relationship that's valuable, not the price tag that comes with the activity.

Simplify birthdays and holidays

Birthdays and holidays: they come around every year. Some people love holidays; others are stressed by these events. However they feel about it, people tend to spend an incredible amount of time, money, and resources celebrating these milestones. It's not necessary. Birthdays and holidays are about honoring an important event, not buying more stuff. Try to remember what the original purpose of the day is.

Religious holidays such as Christmas, Hanukkah, and Easter have become consumer events instead of spiritual remembrances. Even if your family does not celebrate these days as religious holidays, do remember their original intent. Christmas honors the birth of a miracle, Hanukkah is in celebration of the lasting light, and Easter is about the resurrection of the spirit. How can your family best honor these things?

Secular holidays such as Thanksgiving, Halloween, Fourth of July, and Valentine's Day also send us running to the store. Is that really necessary? Can't we give thanks for friends and family, be playful in costume, remember our country's birth, and say, "I love you" to our sweetheart without spending money? Of course.

Look at how you celebrate birthdays and holidays. Decide what's important to you about the event and how you want to honor the day. On Thanksgiving, our family likes to eat food we've raised or grown and then volunteer at a community Thanksgiving meal. During December we light candles and open a homemade Advent calendar each day. On Christmas we exchange gifts: each person gives each other person one present (often homemade, or a personal gift certificate for a special activity). Then we go skiing or sledding. We donate to a local nonprofit in lieu of gifts to extended family. Birthdays are similar: the birthday person gets to choose their meal and type of dessert. There are one or two gifts. If there's a party for friends, it's for getting together and having fun, not for gifts, which is made clear beforehand.

Homemade gifts can run a wide range. Sewn, knitted, or other craft items, baked goods or other special treats, gift certificates for things like massage, breakfast in bed, housecleaning or repairs, framed photographs, a poem — the list is endless. Think of the things your loved ones like to do (or not do, like cleaning or painting, which is handy for gift certificates) and consider what people might like to receive. Even the littlest folk can give a gift certificate for keeping their room clean, or one drawing every month to post on the refrigerator. Use your imagination to help turn the tide of excessive and expensive consumerism.

Be sure to let your extended family (grandparents, siblings, etc.) in on your wish for simpler holidays. This may be a difficult conversation or a welcome one. Too often children of all ages come to expect lots of presents from their parents or grandparents and begin to equate gifts with love. The older generation may become burdened by having to outdo themselves with each visit and each holiday. It may be up to you to stop the parade of unnecessary gifts.

It's nice to have fun on a special day and not be burdened by unwanted junk and unwanted bills, never mind all the trash that comes along with the stuff. Learn to say no to society and the expectations of friends and family, and create new and more frugal rituals for you and your family.

What about pets?

For many people, spending time with their pet brings them great joy and is the epitome of play. But it's important to remember that our pets cost money and consume time and resources just like we do. We feed our pets, provide them with health care, and buy them toys, clothes, and special beds. Some pets live a better life than many people in our country and around the world.

If you want a pet in your life, treat your pet responsibly. Spend time with them, play with them, take them on walks and adventures, spay or neuter them, and don't buy them toys. Just as with babies and toddlers, often the best pet toys are already lying around your house. Watch their health-care consumption, as well. Veterinarians, like medical doctors, may prescribe tests, medications, surgery, and vaccinations just because they think it's a good idea, or that's what they've been taught in school. Ask questions. Find out why they've prescribed a certain test or procedure, whether it's really necessary, and whether there is another way to accomplish the same thing.

Look at the food your pet eats and where it comes from. Is there a way for your pet to eat more healthfully? Your pet doesn't need fancy, expensive food, and you can often find good-quality pet food in bulk at a reasonable price. Some people choose to feed their pets raw poultry purchased locally, which can be cheaper than traditional pet food. Consult your veterinarian about this dietary choice. (At the same time, be sure to prevent your cat from eating too locally — you can bell your feline to warn the songbirds.) Make sure your dogs are well trained. If you choose to have a pet, be sure to look for one at your local animal shelter or Humane Society and forgo purchasing an expensive breed. And when your pet comes to the end of their days, think twice before spending a lot of money and resources on prolonging their life.

Stop paying for entertainment

You have considered how and why you use paid entertainment. Perhaps you know by now what things are important to you and what things aren't. It's time to put into practice what you have learned.

Many times we pay for entertainment because we are

bored, stressed, or think it's good for us or for our family. Everyone wants to learn new things, be entertained, and laugh and cry. There's nothing like a good book, movie, play or concert to make us feel and think new things.

By all means do what is important to you. Just be sure that it is important and that you can't find the same meaning in another, less expensive, way. Pay for it if that makes sense to you, but be thoughtful about your consumption of fun-for-money, whatever it is.

You can often volunteer for organizations and businesses that provide different kinds of fun activities. They usually need people to do mailings, sell tickets, create programs, greet visitors, usher, set up and take down sets, serve refreshments, etc. If you want to attend an event, check in with the people who are putting it on to see if they need your help. Besides being a way to see or do something at no cost, it also allows you to connect with your community and make new friends who share the same interests. It's a great thing for a family or group of friends to do together as well.

If you have a hobby that tends to get expensive, like knitting or quilting, ask your friends to pass along yarn and fabric that they no longer want or use. You can then knit hats for people undergoing chemotherapy or for newborn babies, make quilts for homeless children, or knit cozy shawls for the dying. Just drop these items off with a local school nurse, at a hospital or hospice, or at community action agency. They'll be sure to find a good home for your creative efforts.

Scout yard sales for board games and jigsaw puzzles. Take up cross-country skiing or snowshoeing to avoid the expense of downhill skiing or snowboarding (or volunteer at your local ski area in exchange for a season pass). Take a class or attend a lecture at your local library or other venue that offers free or low-cost events. While you're at the library, check out videos, DVDs, books, and magazines. Learn to create crossword puzzles or do card tricks. Walk around your neighborhood with a bird or plant identification book or a sketch pad. There are many fun things to do for next to nothing.

For other low-cost/no-cost ways to have fun, check out this list.

Walk

Run

Read

Hike

Bike

Snowshoe

Swim

Surf

Kayak

Go sledding

Cross-country ski

Play cards

Play board games

Play Frisbee

Play disc golf

Go roller-skating or ice skating outdoors

Do jigsaw puzzles

Do/create crossword, and other types of, puzzles

Tell stories

Tell jokes

Juggle

Blow bubbles

Make papier mâché creations

Play badminton

Play croquet

Play soccer

Play softball or whiffle ball

Play catch

Shoot hoops

Garden

Write

Have a potluck

Play music

Sing

Identify trees, wildflowers, or birds

Learn something new

Play charades

Draw/sketch

Dance

Take up a craft with recycled materials (knitting, crocheting, quilting, rug making)

Read a play aloud with friends

Cook

Make ice cream without electricity

Repair/refinish/build furniture

Play dress-up

Carve wood

Stand on your head or do cartwheels

Do yoga, tai chi, or qi gong

Play on the playground

Fly a kite

Go to a free concert, play or lecture

Learn a foreign language

Write silly lyrics to popular tunes

Go to a museum on a free-admisson day

Walk your town or city looking at the architecture

Pick berries or apples

Hunt for wild foods

Learn card and magic tricks

Build a tree house or playhouse with recycled materials

Visit your local animal shelter and play with the cats and dogs

Memorize poetry

If you live in or near your state capital, go to your statehouse and watch the legislature in action, or drop in on your city-council meetings

Sit on a bench in an interesting or beautiful place and watch the world go by

12. Travel

For many people, travel is important. We want to experience other places and cultures as a way to learn new things, have a change from our own lives, and have an opportunity to explore the many variations in our world. For some, travel seems ridiculously expensive and only something to be undertaken if you're wealthy or willing to go into debt.

Travel can cost whatever you want it to, however. Certainly, there are plenty of people who choose to travel in luxury, whether or not they can afford it. But it can also be done frugally if you're willing to be creative and experiment with how and when you get there, where you stay, what you eat, and how you pass your time when you're away from home.

Consider how and why you travel

First, think about why you want to travel. Is it a way to keep up with your coworkers — to see who can take the most exotic vacation and brag about it at work? Is it a way to get away from your own life — an escape in every sense of the word? Is it a way to learn more about your avocation — art, history, opera, birds, mountain climbing, or any other interesting pastime? Is it a way to visit family and friends? Is it something to do because that's what you're supposed to want to do?

There are plenty of people who go on vacation to a beach or another popular destination when they would really rather stay home, putter about the garden, and read a stack of good books without worrying about the hassles of air travel or having to keep to someone else's schedule for meals and entertainment, never mind spending all that money. Is that you? Don't travel just because you think that's what people do on their time off from work. You can have fun, relax, and learn new things wherever you are.

Think of your time off as a holiday (holy-day), rather than a vacation. Holidays denote something meaningful, special, and memorable, whereas a vacation sounds like you're trying to get away from your life. Traveling to a new place is sometimes about getting away from it all, but it's also about taking the time to appreciate other places and cultures in a way that will help you appreciate your own.

Travel close to (or at!) home

It's time for your annual vacation. What do you do? Do you jet off to a destination resort, rent a cabin in the mountains or at the shore, visit relatives, hop in your recreational vehicle (RV) for a tour of the country, or pack your backpack and head for the trail? Are these activities fun and fulfilling for you, or do you end up gaining weight, being stressed out, fighting, and worrying about what it's going to cost?

There are many ways to spend your time off from work, ways that are inexpensive and still fun. What would it be like if you stayed home and explored the area where you live? There are probably many beautiful and interesting spots within walking or biking distance of your house. You could plan to treat yourself to a few special home-cooked meals — things that you normally might not have time to make. You could learn to make croissants, bagels, or ice cream, for example. Look around and consider what you might do.

If you love being in or on the water, check out nearby spots for swimming and boating. If you love adventure sports, look into the closest surfing, skiing, rock climbing, or hiking spots. If you love art museums or historic sites, make sure you've visited all the local ones before you venture further afield. There are plenty of people who probably choose your area to visit on holiday. Take the time to look around and see what draws tourists to your town.

Consider the real cost of transportation

Today many people are concerned about the environmental cost of travel in general, and air travel in particular. Whether you get to your destination by plane, train, bus, motorized boat, or car, you are using some of our ever-dwindling supply of oil and adding more carbon dioxide to our already deteriorating atmosphere. Each of these forms of transportation uses a different amount of fuel and creates a different amount of pollution. (Check out www.nativeenergy.com/pages/travel_calculator/30.php to determine the environmental cost of your next trip.) You can purchase carbon offsets if you want, or you can choose to travel a different way.

Just because most people fly wherever they go doesn't mean you have to. Of course, if you want to cross an ocean and don't have a lot of time, a plane is the only practical way to go. One way to save money — and the environmental cost of travel — is to travel less frequently but stay for a longer period of time. Spending a month in Europe or on a Caribbean island every four years instead of a week once a year means one round-trip flight instead of four. It also means you could rent an apartment or condo for that month and pay less for your food and lodging. It means you could save the money in advance and not have to go into debt. It means you could spend the four years learning the language of the country you wish to visit, studying the history and cultural sites, and really making the most of your time there.

If you are traveling closer to home, consider taking the train or a bus instead of driving. It can be much more relaxing to have someone else getting you there while you take the time to look out the window and enjoy the sights. You can also try walking, kayaking, or biking to your destination, or just have your whole holiday be moving through a particular place in a nonmotorized way. You'll see a lot more and learn more about an area by taking it slowly, and you'll save costs, both financially and environmentally.

If you choose motorized transport, be sure to plan ahead and look for bargains on the Internet. Buying tickets in advance is usually cheaper, as is departing and arriving at odd times and going in the off season. Be flexible.

Think about where you lay your head

There are many options for lodging. You don't have to pull off the highway and into the parking lot of the first chain motel you come to. You don't even have to stay in a hotel or motel. You can stay in a bed-and-breakfast, in a campground, in a hostel, in someone's home (stranger or friend), or in a rental house, condo, or apartment. In fact, the choices can be quite overwhelming. After a long day on the road or traipsing around ancient ruins, you may be ready to stop at the first place with a vacancy!

It helps to do your research. Today, almost all forms of lodging can be found on the Internet. Before you leave home, check out places on your route. If you're sticking to a firm itinerary, make reservations before you leave home. If you're not, get an idea of what's available where you are going. Learn which chain motels are in your price range (and sign up for their "regular guest" programs, which will earn you free nights). Or stay at independently owned motels — usually much cheaper than their better-known counterparts. Some of the best motels I've stayed at have been mom-and-pop places. One was in the prairies of Alberta, where a room with two double beds and a full kitchen, and fresh, homemade blueberry muffins in the morning cost a fraction of the chain motel down the road.

If you haven't done your pretrip research, go door-to-door at the selection of motels at your highway exit and find out who has the best price. It will take an extra ten or fifteen minutes of your time, but it will reap financial rewards (so do stop before you're just too exhausted to do this). I've even had a desk clerk offer a lower price as I turned around to head for the door. It's worth it to ask for any possible discounts. If you belong to AAA or AARP, you will probably get a discount, and with AAA you can get free guidebooks that will help you with your motel (and dining, entertainment, and cultural) choices. On one cross-country trip with my teenage children, we used our AAA guidebook every day as we traveled completely spontaneously, never knowing where we would stop. Does a potential motel have in-room coffee makers? Refrigerators? A swimming pool? Is it in our price range? In we'd drive, those being our only criteria for where we slept.

Hostels are no longer just for young people. Most of them now accept, and even cater to, older people and families. You will get a basic room, most likely with toilet and bathing facilities down the hall, and kitchen privileges. If you are a single traveler, you will probably share a room with others of your gender, which can be either good or bad. We've all heard stories of lifelong friendships that began when sharing living quarters while traveling; we've also heard an equal amount of horror stories of drunken and throwing-up roommates, theft, and general disagreeableness. But remember, part of traveling is taking chances and trying something new.

You can trade homes with other people around the world or join an organization that allows you to contact folks who are willing to let you sleep on their couch for a night. There are many organizations now that offer these services. As an example of how this works, check out www.homeexchange.org for home trade options, and www.joomla.servas.org for information about being or finding an international host.

If you like tenting out or prefer to travel by RV, you have a wide selection of campgrounds (and parking lots) available to you. There are national and state parks, privately run facilities, or, for the most frugal, just a private, flat spot in which to pitch a tent (do ask permission if there is a house nearby). And remember, you don't have to own that camping equipment or RV yourself. Try renting or co-owning with a friend.

Eat locally and simply

Many of us love to travel as a way to enjoy new and different foods, but eating out three times a day can start to wear thin and can cost a fortune. You can practice simple, local, and seasonal eating on the road, too.

When my family goes on a trip, we pack our bags with plenty of nutritious snack foods, and one of the first things we do at our destination (or along with way if we're on the road for several days) is find a grocery store to stock up on local fruits, vegetables, breads, and cheeses. Just as with daily trips away from home, be sure to travel with nuts, dried or whole fruit, bread, cheese, water, and something in your thermos. These things can sustain you well through traffic jams, long bike rides, train or bus trips, or airplanes with no (or poor) food service. (If you're flying, fill your empty water bottle from a water fountain after you go through security.)

Bring along a small cooler for things that are perishable. Before you leave, you can freeze water in a plastic container to place in the cooler, and refill it with ice along the way to keep things cool. For a longer stay somewhere, ask to have a refrigerator in your room. (Many inexpensive motels now have microwaves and refrigerators in every room.)

A small electric pot designed for boiling water can also be used to make soup or cook vegetables or grains. Check your local hardware store for this handy, inexpensive item. You can also use it at home for boiling water for coffee or tea. It uses much less fuel than boiling water on your kitchen range.

While you're packing, don't forget eating utensils (get a "spork" for every member of the family — it's a spoon, knife, and fork in one utensil), a sharp knife, your favorite condiments, and a dishtowel or napkin or two. Bring bowls and mugs as well if you're driving. Bring a small mess kit if you're on public transportation.

When you reach your destination (or if your journey is your destination), do eat out now and then. Trying the local cuisine is important, especially if you're in a foreign country. Look for inexpensive restaurants and street vendors for good food. Be adventuresome and look for foods that you can't find at home and that are made with local ingredients, wherever you are. Lunch is usually your best deal — you often get the same meal as is served at dinner, for a much lower price. Try limiting your eating out to once every two or three days, and really enjoy yourself. Skip the chain fast-food places. You didn't go to Europe to eat at McDonald's or Kentucky Fried Chicken.

Pack light

There's nothing worse than lugging around a heavy suitcase (or two) over cobblestone streets, up and down elevators, stairs, and escalators, and along busy sidewalks. Whether you will be gone a week or a month, you will need very few clothes and just the bare minimum of toiletries. With a carry-on bag or backpack, you'll have more flexibility and more fun, and you won't have to pay checked-luggage fees.

If you're headed to a hot climate, a few T-shirts, a pair or two of shorts, a dress or nice slacks and shirt for going out, a lightweight sweater for chilly evenings, some rain gear, a bathing suit, underwear, sandals, and basic toiletries are all you need. For a trip to colder climates, a couple of long-sleeve shirts or turtlenecks, a couple of pairs of pants, a winter version of your dress or slacks and shirt for going out, a wool sweater, a warm coat (for either snow or rain), sturdy walking shoes that can handle the weather, underwear, and basic toiletries are enough.

Don't forget to bring any medicine you take regularly, along with a small amount of OTC pain medication and also some antidiarrheal medication if you're headed to a destination where you might run into questionable food or water. Bring sunscreen as well, a hat if you're especially sensitive to the sun, and insect repellant if the mosquitos might spoil your trip. Keep your personal-care products simple: toothbrush, paste, and floss, shampoo, soap, body lotion, and a brush or comb. Don't forget shaving equipment, if you use it, and contact-lens supplies (or wear your glasses for the trip and leave all that stuff at home.) You're out to relax and enjoy your surroundings, so leave the cosmetics, hair-styling products, and fancy jewelry behind, if you use them at all.

If you're traveling with children, let them choose one small toy or game, a ball or a Frisbee, and a few favorite books (which they'll carry in their own backpack). There's no need to bring along lots of things to entertain them: the trip is supposed to do that.

Leave the electronics at home, too. It's not a holiday if you have your laptop and your BlackBerry with you. Not only are they heavy to carry, they're also prone to theft.

If you like to write, consider bringing a small notebook to be your travel journal. If you like to draw, bring a small sketch pad. If you like to take photographs, bring your camera. Otherwise, leave these things at home.

If you're backpacking, kayaking, or biking, you'll definitely want to travel light. You don't need a lot of special clothes and equipment to do this. Just bring the same basic clothes and toiletries as above (depending on the climate you'll travel through), along with appropriate footwear and rain gear, food, a small stove, a mess kit, a guidebook or map, and a sleeping bag, mat, and tent if you're going to bed down outdoors.

Go to places off the beaten track

Everyone (it seems) wants to go to the big-name cities such as New York, San Francisco, Paris, Rome, or Tokyo or the destination resorts in the Bahamas, Hawaii, Mexico, the Caribbean, or the Mediterranean. These places can be very expensive, though.

If you want to explore ancient Roman ruins, see great art, or eat fabulous food, you can go to any number of smaller European cities. If you want to lay on a beach and do nothing for a week, there are many beaches all over the world that are cheaper and less crowded than the famous resorts. There may even be one a short distance from your home.

You can also skip the better-known European countries like France and Italy for lesser-known and less expensive countries like Portugal, the Czech Republic, or Romania. Same goes with Central and South America, Africa, and Asia. Look into lesser-known areas. (Do check for travel warnings at www.travel.state.gov/travel if you plan to travel abroad.)

Wherever you want to go, consider why you're intrigued with that place and see if there's a less expensive destination that will fulfill your particular interest. Do your research and it will pay off.

Go in the off-season

Another way to save money is to go when very few other people are going. Travel to the Caribbean islands during hurricane season, Scandinavia or Russia in the depths of winter, or south of the equator during the Northern Hemisphere's summer. You'll find fewer tourists, a better chance to meet the locals, and a much less expensive trip. Transportation and lodging will be cheaper, and museums or other special sites will have reduced rates (and possibly reduced hours, so be sure to check).

Don't be afraid to take your children out of school to travel abroad in the cheaper winter months. Talk to your children's teachers about the work they'll need to do to keep up, and plan what in particular they can learn and bring back to their classmates. My parents took me out of school for a month-long trip when I was in eighth grade. My requirement was to speak to all the geography classes when I returned about where I'd been and what I'd seen. That was education enough! If you've chosen to home-school, you can do a whole project about your destination — before and after the trip — and have the flexibility to go when you please.

Respect the culture you're in

When I travel abroad, I can almost always tell the Americans: they're the ones in athletic shoes and inappropriate clothing talking in loud voices and generally being rude. Fortunately, there are plenty of other Americans who aren't doing that: I can't tell who they are!

If you are going to a culture that is different from ours, respect it. Don't wear jeans and T-shirts with political or potentially offensive sayings. Dress in a more subdued way than you might at home. Be particularly aware of the importance of modest dress in the Middle East and other very religious areas. They don't appreciate seeing bare arms and bare legs, especially on a woman.

Keep your voice down and do learn some of the local language, even if it's just "please," "thank you," "I'm sorry," "hello," and "goodbye." Watch how people in hotels and shops speak to you and mimic what they do. In France, for example, it is considered rude to ask for something in a store or place of lodging without first saying, "Bonjour." No business can be transacted without that particular social grace. Don't expect that everyone will speak some English, either. Use gestures or written numbers and drawings to communicate if neither of you speaks the other's language.

If you're touring a cathedral, mosque, synagogue, or other religious building, keep quiet out of respect for any services going on, other sightseers who want to feel the peace of the space, and anyone who is praying or participating in other devotional activities.

If you have children with you, make sure they respect the same rules. If they're too rambunctious to be quiet, take them to a park or playground to run around and blow off steam. It's a great place for them to meet local children, too. You'd be amazed at how well kids can communicate even when they don't speak the same language. The parents might have the opportunity to meet other parents, and it will be a richer experience for everyone. By blending in with the locals and doing what they do, you'll have a greater opportunity to meet people and experience the culture first-hand.

Before you go, read about the places you plan to visit and learn about any particular customs and rituals you need to know. It's best to be prepared and save yourself hassle and embarrassment. Loud, inappropriately dressed foreigners are not only offensive to local people, they're also targets for theft, scams, and pickpockets. If you're a victim of crime while traveling, your trip will suddenly get much more expensive.

Take advantage of free museums, concerts, and other cultural activities

Every major museum around the world usually has a particular day of the week or month, or time of day, when there is no admission fee. Take advantage of this. You don't need to pay through the nose to enjoy music around the world; there are many choices available to you. Cathedrals may have free organ or choir concerts, and there are always street musicians, free concerts in parks, clubs and bars with no cover charge, and the chance opportunity to overhear the music being played for weddings or other events.

Many people like to stroll around old cemeteries, wander down twisty streets looking at the architecture, walk along a river or canal and look at the boats, or simply sit on a bench and watch the scene that passes them by. All of this can be done for free.

Find out at your place of lodging, or at the local tourist information office, what's going on in the area you are visiting. There may be cooking demonstrations, lectures, fairs, fireworks, celebrations for a public holiday, parades, or athletic events. Keep your eyes open for fun things to do for free that will help you learn about where you are. Don't be cheap, though: if there's something you really want to see or do that has an admission fee, pay it, and enjoy yourself.

Beware of gift shops

Traveling should not be an excuse for buying things that you don't really want or need. You don't need souvenirs to help you remember your trip, and your friends and relatives don't need them either. Hearing your stories and seeing your photos or sketches will be more meaningful than a T-shirt that says "Bangkok" on it.

On the other hand, many lovely and delicious things are only made in certain parts of the world. If you want to buy a piece of Limoges china, some Andean weaving, a few yards of Southeast Asian silk, or a couple of bottles of South African wine, by all means do so. Just make sure that it is something you really want and have room for in your life, that you can get it home safely (and that you are allowed to transport it in the first place), and that you've paid a reasonable price for it.

Keep a journal

A way to be sure to remember all the details of your trip inexpensively is to record them as you go along. What you saw and what you did, where you stayed and what you ate, and the feelings that came up as you experienced this new place can be written down in a journal. Encourage your children to keep journals, too. For those who can draw, a sketch pad can record many of the same activities, thoughts, and feelings.

Besides holding memories, your journal can be used to track your expenses for the journey and help you remember the name of that little hotel you loved, or the restaurant with the wonderful pizza, so you can tell a friend who plans to travel to the same place, or remember it if you ever go there again yourself. Your journals will also be important keepsakes for your descendants. Foreign travel will be very different in the future. Just as we love to read of transatlantic crossings and African safaris that took place over a hundred years ago, people in the future will want to read our reflections on a particular place at a particular time.

Journals will stand the test of time. A stack of photographs of nameless monuments, cathedrals, mountains, and beaches won't.

Volunteer

A great way to learn about a country, place, or culture is to volunteer. You can do this in your own country or abroad. There are many organizations that can help place you in different kinds of situations. Most groups ask that you pay your own transportation costs, and some request a small amount for room and board. Beware of organizations that ask you to pay excessively for the privilege of helping out.

You don't have to go too far afield to volunteer. Many of our national and state parks have a way for you to volunteer clearing trails or repairing buildings in exchange for free use of the park. You can go to the site of a disaster, such as the 2004 Asian tsunami, Hurricane Katrina, or the 2010 Haitian earthquake, to help rebuild. Be sure to do this through a reputable national or international organization such as the Red Cross or Habitat for Humanity, or check with the disaster-response group of your religious faith.

You can join Willing Workers on Organic Farms (WWOOF: www.wwoof.org) and spend a week or two planting, weeding, and harvesting in almost any country around the world. You can join Volunteers for Peace (www.vfp.org) and work with others from all over the planet on small crews building playgrounds, creating nature trails, refurbishing old buildings, and other such hands-on activities.

There are many great ways to have a "working" holiday. Volunteering not only feels good, it allows us to interact with people and places in a way we might never have the opportunity to otherwise.

Be flexible

Above all, be flexible. Don't always stick to a planned itinerary, a high season, or an over-run location. Be prepared for new, cheaper, and better food, lodging, and transportation possibilities. Be prepared for sudden illness or injury. Be prepared for a traveling companion to say, "I've had enough. Let's stay put for a few days." (Or, "Let's get out of here.") Keep an open mind. There will be travel delays, disappointing hotels and meals, tired feet, upset tummies, and overwhelmed senses.

Take care of yourself when you're on the road. Don't push yourself too much, but don't hold back either. Eat well, sleep enough, and watch your caffeine and alcohol intake. If you're ready for any twist of fate (good or bad) or unexpected opportunity, you'll have a lot more fun, and your trip will be richer and more frugal for it.

13. Money

Money. We love it and we hate it. We assign all kinds of nonmonetary values to money: it will bring us love, it is a sign of our success, it is how we care for our family, it is dirty. In truth, money is nothing more than something we exchange our life energy for, whether that money comes to us from employment, investments, disability or Social Security benefits, inheritance, child support, or gambling.

How do you feel about money? Do you have enough? Do you even know how much is enough? Do you have debt, small or large? Do you use money to buy happiness, entertainment, and prestige? Or are you miserly, saving every penny, never purchasing anything you really want, and never donating anything to charity? Think about your relationship with money.

In our society we can never completely function without being part of the cash economy. We cannot barter for our utility bills or property taxes (at least not yet!), but there are many ways we can reduce our reliance on cash, credit cards, and our paycheck. By understanding our individual financial picture and how we use money to get what we want and need, we will have a better idea of how to spend, and not spend, that precious resource.

There are many ways to look at your money, how you earn it, how you spend it, how you save it, how you invest it, and what it can and cannot do for you.

Here are some ways to help you understand your relationship with money and how best to use it.

Figure out your net worth

Once you have taken an inventory of everything you own (Chapter Nine: Stuff), it's time to bring out the pieces of paper that list your worldly possessions and their monetary value. Now get another piece of scrap paper and list the big stuff you own like the vehicle(s), the boat(s), and the house. Make sure that everything you own is now in black and white, with a monetary value attached. Add it up. If you owe the bank money on any of these items, subtract what you owe (principal plus interest) from the price the thing would get in today's market.

On another piece of paper write down all your financial instruments and assets like savings and checking accounts, certificates of deposit, individual retirement accounts, stocks, bonds, pension plans, or rental property.

On another paper, list all your other debts (besides the house and the car) such as credit-card debt, student loans, home-equity loans, personal loans, and unpaid bills.

Add it all up — the worth of your house, your belongings, any vehicles or boats, your financial assets. Then subtract the debts, and you will have a total for your current net worth. It may be a large, or a small, number. It may be a negative number. But it will be your number. This number will help you understand what financial freedom you may already have or if there are some things you want to change.

Make a plan to get out of debt

Personal debt in North America is spiraling out of control. We are taught from an early age that it is healthy and good to borrow money. It shows that we are mature, responsible, and have good credit. We can deduct our mortgage interest, and other forms of credit interest, on our taxes. This is the American way, right?

At this point, it seems to be, but it doesn't have to be. Being in debt costs you money: significant amounts of money, in many cases. It also costs you emotionally, physically, and spiritually when you worry about it, ignore it and accumulate more, or work at a job you hate simply to pay the bills. You can get out of debt — many people have, quite successfully and easily — by making a plan.

Only you know what it is you actually owe. As part of your plan to get out of debt, make your first step not getting into further debt. Cut up your credit cards if credit-card debt is an issue. Stop any escalating consumer spending and debt, then pay off your credit-card debt, as it, no doubt, has the highest interest rate. (Talk to your credit-card company about the best way to do this; sometimes they are willing to forgive some debt.)

Look at your mortgage, if you have one. Can you sell your current home and move into a smaller, less expensive house and get rid of your house debt? Look at your car loan, if you have one (or two or more). Can you pay it off quickly, or sell your current vehicle and purchase a less expensive one, or do without a car at all? Do the same for educational loans, personal loans, and any other outstanding debt you may have.

Once you get out of debt and start saving money, you will have more freedom and peace of mind. That itself is worth more than you can imagine.

Keep track of your income and expenses

I have found that keeping a record of all your income and expenses is one of the most significant things you can do to understand many aspects of your life. You will find out what things you tend to buy unconsciously, things you may not really want and need. You will find out if the way you spend money corresponds to your values. You will find out exactly how much you pay for takeout coffee, car expenses, fast food, new clothes, and a myriad of other choices. However, you will never find out these things unless you keep track and review your income/expense statements monthly. Your checkbook register and your credit-card bill will give you part of the story, if you have such luxuries in your life. To get the full story of how you spend your money, however, you have to keep track of everything. This is not a budget (planning how you will spend money before you spend it), but a reflection of how you actually spent your money.

Some of us love charts, graphs, and lists. For others, this may seem like an onerous chore, but the amount of information and personal "ahas" you will get from keeping track is immeasurable.

Find a system that works for you. I ask for receipts from the rest of my family, and then I write these amounts on a sheet of paper as they come up. (Don't save all your receipts to write down once a month; do it daily or several times a week.) Other people choose to keep an index card or small notebook in their pocket or purse on which to list each expenditure. You will need to find a way that makes sense for your life.

At the end of each month, tally items in general categories such as food, transportation, clothing, household, and entertainment. You will need to create your own categories, for only you can know your own life. My category lists have changed over the years as my life, my interests, and my living situations have changed. Some people choose to do this on the computer, but I am happy keeping track on paper. Do what works best for you.

Over time, you will gain a picture of where your money goes. Equally important is keeping track of the money that comes into your life, and where it comes from. Some will be earned income from a job. Other income may be from bank interest, child support, gifts, dividends, rebates and refunds, or governmental benefits.

Each month you will get a snapshot of your life: where your money comes from and where it goes. You will see the costs associated with your job (lunches out, certain clothes, day care, commuting costs), the costs associated with your children (toys, clothes, school supplies), the costs associated with your home (rent or mortgage, upkeep, taxes, utilities, furniture), and other costs incurred in day-to-day living: food, entertainment, gifts, donations, impulse purchases, pet food, clothing, health care, etc.

This snapshot will tell you what is important to you and what isn't. Ask yourself if spending twenty dollars a month on mints, a hundred on takeout coffee, or two hundred on alcohol is really worth it to you. Look at what you purchased, what you gave away, and what you earned, and see how it all fits together. Does your balance sheet balance? Does your balance sheet reflect your values? Are there some things you could do without? Are your job-related expenses rivaling your job-related income? Are there some things you could get for less or no money?

Use cash and stop the credit-card habit

Whether or not you are burdened with credit-card debt, it's best to use cash and not credit cards. Credit-card companies are making a lot of money from their customers, both the people who use the cards who end up paying exorbitant amounts in fees and interest, as well as the businesses who accept them (they also pay fees, often 3 percent of the price of your purchase). Credit-card use drives up the prices of the items you buy as the stores try to simply recover the fees they have to pay. You end up paying twice.

Using cash may also help you spend less money or be more thoughtful as you reach for your wallet. Cash is real: the bills and coins in your hand, the change you are given at the register. It's more real than the little plastic card swiped through the machine and the little slip of paper you receive. If you have children, they'll learn more about money by handling cash than by using plastic.

Unfortunately, credit cards are usually required for some online purchases, such as tickets, hotel reservations, etc. Feel free to have a card on hand for emergencies like this, but don't use it for everyday purchases that can be bought with cash.

If you're not convinced ("Credit cards are so much simpler to use." "I don't want to carry all that cash." "But I earn frequent-flyer miles/store discounts/free stuff with my card!"), then watch the movie *Maxed Out*, which chronicles our spiraling problems with debt and credit-card use.

Beware of hidden fees

Credit cards are not the only things with hidden fees. ATMs may have fees, savings and checking accounts may have fees, other accounts held by a stockbroker or other investment advisor may have fees. Be sure to ask when you open any kind of account with stores, banks, credit unions, and other financial institutions.

Open a savings account and use it

It is important to put aside a portion of your income on a regular basis to use for emergencies, future purchases, travel, and anything else you might want to do. Call it your Freedom Fund. Instead of going into debt to buy something — or to feed your family in case you lose your job — you will have the peace of mind that comes from knowing your bills (and more) can be paid by cash on hand.

Plan on saving and holding onto the equivalent of six to twelve months' worth of living expenses in case calamity befalls you or your family. The interest paid on savings accounts has fluctuated widely over the years, so the purpose of this account is not necessarily to produce income but rather to have security. Once you have more than the six to twelve months of living expenses set aside, you can then save (and prudently invest) the extra money to use for those things that are meaningful to you. Open savings accounts for your children, as well, and encourage them to save a portion of whatever income they have.

Take a shopping moratorium

The fastest way to save money is to not spend it in the first place. Try not spending any money beyond what you need to pay for your home (rent/mortgage/taxes and utilities), basic food, commuting and required work-related expenses, and any debt service you may have. That means no clothes, paid entertainment, eating out, hair cuts, or impulse purchases for a time period you choose — a week, a month, or a year. See what it feels like to want something and then have to say no. Ask yourself why you wanted it. Ask yourself if you could get it another way, without spending money. Learn to understand your need to entertain yourself by shopping, having new things, and paying other people to bring you happiness. Be sure to bank what you don't spend during your shopping moratorium in your Freedom Fund!

Consider how and why you work for money, and the real cost of having that job

Money does not just go out of our lives, it also comes in, primarily from whatever kind of work we do. Think about your job: Do you like it? Is it in line with your values? Do you come home stressed out or refreshed? Is your salary or hourly wage appropriate for the work that you do? Are you valued at your workplace?

Think about the costs associated with having your job. Do you have to wear special clothes? Do you have a long or expensive commute? Does your job require your family to own a second car? Are you expected to subscribe to certain professional journals, attend conferences on your own dime, take extra time (and money) to wine and dine clients, or supply your classroom with paper and pencils? How much do you spend on lunches out, coffee from the downstairs coffee shop, day care for your kids, the hours in the therapist's office or with the masseuse dealing with all your stress, or the six-pack of beer you drink every evening?

Write it all down and add it up. Compare it to the amount on your paycheck. You may find that you're really not making much money at all. If that's true, consider finding another job that won't cost you as much, or, if you have a spouse who is working, don't work for money at all. By staying home, raising your kids yourself, gardening, and taking care of all those household chores you're paying someone else to do, your family may be able to save even more money than if you were working.

Do it yourself

Whether it's changing the oil in your car, doing your taxes, washing your windows, cleaning your house, taking care of your kids, mending your clothes, or cooking your food, learn to do it yourself. The more you can do yourself, the less money you will have to spend to have someone else take care of the basic needs of your life.

Not all of us have the skills to do all of these things, or even want them. But there are many things that we pay other people to do for us without even thinking. Many home repairs and maintenance activities require little skill, just the time and energy to do it. Others will require some training. Ask a friend to help you, or the nice staff at your local hardware, car parts, or craft supply stores.

If you're all thumbs, or are physically unable to do certain tasks, take up bartering.

Learn to barter

Not all of us can do everything, but we can all do something. What are your skills? What are the things you feel you have no chance of learning, let alone mastering? Find out what your friends and neighbors can do, and learn to trade services.

If you're good at sewing, let people know that. Perhaps you'd like someone to cut your hair in exchange for clothing repair. Maybe you're useless with household repairs, but great at cooking. Maybe your neighbor, who hates to cook, would exchange meals for cleaning your house, tuning your bike, or fixing your leaky toilet. For those who have no skill at gardening or household activities, perhaps you can trade child care, pet sitting, computer jobs, or errand services with your more handy neighbors.

Many communities also have formal barter exchange services often referred to as an alternative form of currency or a time bank. People exchange services of all kinds, from house cleaning to clothing repair, small carpentry jobs to rides to the airport. Time banks may also include professionals such as lawyers, dentists, electricians, massage therapists, and alternative health-care providers who are willing to exchange services with nonprofessionals. (Check out www.timebanking.org for more information.) Sign up with one (or start one) in your town. Even if you don't have a time bank in your community, you can simply ask the professionals you do use if they would be willing to barter their services.

Consider the kinds of insurance you have and why you have them

Many people feel that they must be fully covered by insurance, but what is the insurance for? If you have a life-insurance policy to cover the cost of your mortgage and the disposal of your body, perhaps you would consider paying off your mortgage and planning for simple and low-cost care after you are gone, instead. Vehicle liability insurance is generally required by law, but collision insurance isn't; how carefully do you drive? If you don't have a mortgage, homeowner's insurance is not required; how safe do you feel in your home? I've already mentioned health insurance and the different services that that may cover. Then there is long-term-care insurance, travel insurance, rental-car insurance, disability insurance, dental insurance, pet health insurance — just ask the insurance industry: there are policy choices galore.

Having insurance is a choice. Look at your policies, what they cover, and how much they cost. Is there another way to get what you want or need without insurance? Understand that, in many cases, what you may expect to be covered by your insurance policy turns out to be excluded. Read the fine print and ask questions of your insurance agent. That's what they're there for. If you choose to have insurance of whatever kind, be sure to get the best policy for your needs, and at the best price.

Invest your money wisely and responsibly

Once you're out of debt and spending less on the necessities of life, and you have that six to twelve months of living expenses set aside in a savings account, you can look into other forms of investment for your extra cash.

There are many books that explain the various investment vehicles in our society, so it's best that you educate yourself. Visit your library and peruse the finance books. Look for *The Only Investment Guide You'll Ever Need* (Andrew Tobias, Harcourt, 2002) for no-nonsense and unbiased advice. As our economy changes, keep track of new investment choices and challenges. You don't need to hire a stockbroker or investment advisor to do this for you.

Once you feel you understand your options, put your money somewhere safe where it can grow and can eventually provide you with enough of an income that you no longer need to work at a job to support yourself and your family (whether that's at the traditional retirement age or not). Remember that most people in our world live on a few dollars a day or less. If you are living frugally in a fulfilling, thoughtful, and respectful way, you may find you don't need a very large income to provide for the needs you must pay for in cash.

Being out of debt and having a cushion in the bank and a steady stream of income from safe investments will bring you incredible peace of mind and amazing freedom.

Be sure to share some of your wealth

Don't forget those who are less fortunate than you. Be sure to donate some portion of your income to your favorite nonprofit organization(s). In addition to cash donations, also volunteer your time. These organizations can use your help stuffing envelopes, making phone calls, fundraising, cleaning their bathrooms, and tending their flowers. Find out how you can best be of use.

Always ask yourself "Is there a way to get what I want for little or no money?"

You are learning how to balance what you need and want in order to have a fulfilling life with spending and saving your money. When you want something — whether it's a quiet dinner with your spouse, a new quilt, a warm sweater, a fun time with your children, or the supplies for your favorite hobby — ask yourself if you can get what you want for little or no money. You can make it yourself, you can check out the list of no-cost/low-cost fun things to do (Chapter Eleven: Fun), you can volunteer or barter in exchange for the item or service, you can use the library. As a friend of mine says, "There are at least five solutions to every problem." Be imaginative; look for creative solutions.

Follow the *Your Money or Your Life* program

Many of the ideas in this chapter come from Vicki Robin's powerful nine-step program, which brings you financial intelligence, integrity, and independence. Check your library for a copy of *Your Money or Your Life*.

14. Children

Many families seeking freedom through frugality wonder and worry about how this will affect their children. One website estimates that, in 2001, it cost between $125,000 and $250,000 to raise a child to age 18, education excluded (www.moneycentral.msn.com). So is it even possible to live frugally with children? If you can figure out how, will your children be ostracized by their peers, be made fun of, feel deprived, or be deprived? Is it fair to impose our values on our children? These are legitimate concerns, like many that we have as caring parents. We want the best for our children; we want them to have fulfilling and fun lives in the security of a loving family.

What better way to accomplish that than by teaching them how to be frugal, to respect their things, to know that they can get what they want without spending a lot of money, and to understand that it's not always necessary to buy every new thing that comes along?

Children, by nature, want to learn all about the world, what's in it, who's in it, what there is to do, and how to be in relation to all of it. It's our job as parents to help them learn all of this. The schools do some, yes, but our children's first and primary teachers are the adults they live with.

Kids tease each other for being different. Adults can do that as well, on their own level. One of our jobs as parents is to teach our children to stand up for themselves in an appropriate way and not to make fun of others for any reason. If your children are not yet born, or are infants or toddlers, you have an opportunity to make new choices without too much stress on the kids. As long as they are warm, sheltered, loved, dry, and fed, they won't care what kind of house they live in, what kind of clothes they wear, what kind of toys they have, and whether they go to the store in a backpack or in a child seat on the back of a bicycle rather than in a car. School-age kids and teens can be more of a challenge, but they are also old enough to understand and to help.

Kids are very good at sensing if their parents are trying to coerce them into something that's "good for them." As you start to move toward a more frugal way of life, talk to your kids. Explain it to them, without condescension, in whatever way is usual for your family. Some families have family meetings, others chat about what's happening in their lives over dinner, at bedtime, or on a Saturday morning. Do what's right for your family, and don't make a big deal about it. Children learn the most by watching their parents' behavior and activities. "Do as I say and not as I do" doesn't cut it with most kids I know.

No one likes change, least of all kids who are in a routine about food, leisure activities, friends, school, and their home/room/stuff. As you make changes, involve your children in a way that is appropriate for their age. Kids can help de-clutter and help set up and run a yard sale (especially if you let them keep the profits). Many kids love to cook and be involved with what their parents are doing (especially the eight-and-under set). A mathematically minded child can keep track of the car's mileage as you gradually cut down on driving. An athletic child may love to start riding bikes everywhere or organize fun things to do with the family that don't involve computers or television. An Internet-savvy child can research energy-saving options or green-building techniques. A relationship-minded child can get the neighbors and their friends involved.

Here are some things to consider as you and your children create a frugal life together.

Learn to say "no"

Your greatest challenge — and greatest gift — for your child is to say "no" to them and mean it. Don't say "no" to everything or to reasonable requests. Think before you say "no," and plan to follow through. Sometimes it's not that we parents forget to say "no" but that we say it too often, without thinking, and our kids learn to ignore us and keep right on going. Then when something really important comes along, they're in the habit of ignoring us. Use "no" judiciously, but firmly.

We all need to learn to say no to many things. Consumerism, excessive TV and computer use, substance abuse, overeating, unhealthy relationships — the list goes on and on. It's OK to say no to designer clothes, television, and junk food just as you would to inappropriate behaviors such as hitting, lying, and drug and alcohol use. Your children need help from you to understand appropriate boundaries about all kinds of things. If you remember that frugality is about respect for time and money, and that a life of frugality will bring freedom to do what is important to you, the conversations will be easier.

When you do choose to say no to something that affects everyone in the family, watch for blanket pronouncements or judgments (i.e., "we're all going to be vegetarian from now on"). It works better, and you're more apt to get buy-in from the younger generation, if you share your ideas first, get their opinions, and make a plan that works for the whole family. In the vegetarian example above, as a place to start, you could have a conversation about factory farming and the amount of land and water that is needed to raise meat, the high cost of animal foods compared to plant foods, and your wish to eat less meat. As an adult you can choose to eat no meat, but if your kids balk, perhaps you can choose to only eat locally and humanely raised meat, and then only once or twice a week. Over time, the kids may be fine with a vegetarian or even vegan diet.

There will be many choices ahead for you as a family. Make each choice thoughtfully, with respect for every family member, and things will go better.

Learn to say "yes" in creative ways

Being frugal is not about denying your children new toys, opportunities to experience new places and cultures, or a chance to learn a new sport. Being frugal is about understanding what it is you and they really want and then figuring out a way to get it without spending a lot of money.

If your child asks for a new toy, find out if they're bored with what they have, if they've heard about the new toy from a friend, or if they simply want some attention from you. If they're bored with what they have, talk about what might interest them; maybe you could build a treehouse together, put together a scrapbook of drawings and photos, find out if they'd like to learn to play a musical instrument, or go to a few yard sales to look for a new game or jigsaw puzzle. If they've heard about the new toy from a friend, talk with them about how each family is different and how everyone doesn't have to do or be the same. If you think they just want some attention from you, find a way to spend time together.

Taking up a new sport or musical instrument doesn't have to cost a lot of money. Used equipment and instruments are easy to come by, and you can often barter for lessons. Traveling can also be done on the cheap, or your family can be armchair travelers by using books, magazines, and DVDs found at your library. New clothes can come from a thrift shop, rummage sale, consignment store, or from your sewing machine (a perfect time to teach your child to sew!).

Look upon becoming a frugal family as an adventure and a puzzle to be figured out together. Your children may have even more creative ideas than you have. Talk with them about some of the things each family member wants, and see if, together, you can come up with a frugal way to get them.

Find ways to have fun together without television

I have already mentioned cutting back on, and eventually getting rid of, your TV. It may be one of the best things you can do for your kids. There are many books and articles on the subject of the unhealthy aspects of TV, but, in my mind, the biggest problems with staring at a flickering screen for hours on end are that it is a big waste of time, and that it can make us feel bad about our lives. We watch stressful national and international news, relentless commercials touting products that no one actually needs, and people having lives we'll never have, wearing beautiful clothes, living in fancy houses, and having interesting relationships. Reality is usually sorely skewed (especially on reality shows). Is this how we want our kids to learn about the world?

I can hear the uproar now: No TV?! How will our kids fit in if they don't watch TV? What about all those educational shows? Besides, it's such a great babysitter.

Is this how we want to raise our children? By parking them in front of a TV? Don't we want them to spend time learning about themselves and the world by playing make-believe, building houses and cities out of blocks, climbing trees, and romping around the yard with their friends? We certainly don't need TV to expand our horizons: educational material can be found the old-fashioned way, in books, through travel, and by experiencing things directly. As with any habit, it can be tough to break the TV one at first. Have patience. Eventually, it will make sense for all of you.

Think of all the time you'll have then to do things, both as individuals and together as a family. Evenings spent reading aloud, playing board games, or creating puzzles, Lego creations, or dollhouses are way more fun than sitting in front of a money-, energy-, and resource-wasting box. Revisit the no-cost/low-cost list of fun things to do (Chapter Eleven: Fun), and you're sure to find a place to start.

Create simple birthdays and holidays

I've also already discussed simplifying birthdays and holidays, but even the most frugal adults usually feel they have to go all out for the kids. For some of us, our best childhood memories are of birthday and holiday celebrations. For others of us, those memories may not be so good. Whatever our memories, we want our children to have wonderful family celebrations. They can be expensive, though, and use too many resources, promote consumerism, and detract from the original meaning of the event. What to do?

Keep it simple. Birthdays don't have to involve big parties with clowns, live animals, and rented tents and games. The December holidays don't have to put you in debt. Ask your kids what they love best about their birthday, the December holidays, and any other holidays your family celebrates. When it comes to the December holidays, for example, find out if it's making cut-out star and reindeer cookies, frying latkes, visiting relatives, having time off from school, singing carols, or attending religious services. Maybe they like having an opportunity to eat their favorite foods, see their cousins, or give other people gifts. You won't know unless you ask.

This is also a good time to say "no" if they get an expensive and consumeristic birthday idea. Having a couple of friends over for a sleepover might be more appealing than twenty or thirty kids playing games and eating junk food for a couple of hours. If your child is social and wants a big party with lots of people, invite whole families and make it a potluck with everyone sharing their favorite board or yard game.

When your child is invited to another child's party, you will be faced with finding a gift for the birthday boy or girl. There are many things you can do besides go out and purchase a brand-new toy. Perhaps your child has something that they would like to give their friend. Maybe you could scout yard sales or thrift shops for something appropriate. If someone in your family has craft skills, a knitted hat, a wooden picture frame (with photo), or some home-sewn doll clothes would be nice. Or try the gift-certificate approach, depending on the child's interests: give the gift of a day at the lake, a day in the mountains, a day at the art museum, or a day at the local science center. Be creative, and if you feel you have to buy something new, be sure to spend what seems right for your budget.

Within the family, limit holiday gifts to one per person. Have each child think long and hard about the one thing that would be most meaningful to them. Opening just a few gifts and then having the whole day or weekend to do other things as a family can be so much more fun and relaxing. As a pleasant side effect, the adults won't have to worry about big bills come January.

Teach them to cook

I am continually amazed at the number of people who don't know how to cook. Microwaves and fast food have made basic household food preparation with a conventional stovetop and oven a thing of the past. Reclaim it! There are few activities that children find more fun than cooking. If you don't like cooking, you might find, as a bonus, that someone in the younger generation may have a gift for it.

Start when they're little. Stirring batter, cracking eggs, using an eggbeater, measuring chocolate chips and oatmeal for cookies, reading recipes, and chopping vegetables are all activities that kids of almost any age can do. Sit them up on the counter or pull over a stool, and be prepared to make a mess.

If you don't know how to cook, you can learn together.

They'll be amazed at what they can create. They'll begin to feel confident in the kitchen and equate cooking with good times. They'll be whipping up noodles, scrambled eggs, and grilled cheese sandwiches by the time they're seven or eight. They'll serve you a multicourse meal by the time they're teenagers and will love to make tasty desserts for their friends. They'll be self-reliant in this area and always able to fend for themselves, and you won't be stuck with all the food preparation. Learning to cook is a gift that keeps on giving.

Raise your children yourself

One of the largest expenses for many families with young children is the cost of day care and after-school care. Many parents assume there is no other way to handle those hours when they are at work and the children need to be looked after. You actually have several options.

First, calculate how much money it costs you directly to have someone else watch your children. Then add in any additional costs such as mileage and car use to get to the day-care center, extra fees, food, diapers, and other things that may be required for you to purchase that you might not necessarily use at home. Somehow figure in the lost hours when everyone is sick because of a bug brought home from day care. You may discover that it's actually cheaper for one parent to not work at all.

If no one wants to give up their job to stay home with the kids full time, each parent could look into working part time or changing their hours so they could coordinate to cover child care. Perhaps this is the time to start a home business (which the kids could help with), or telecommute. You don't always have to do these things from nine to five either. You may be able to work early mornings before everyone is up, during nap time, or in the evening when the other parent is home. You may be able to find another family in a similar situation and take turns watching each other's children. Be creative about this if you find that day care is eating up too much of your money.

Consider homeschooling

I couldn't imagine letting another adult have the joy of watching my children learn to walk, talk, or read, so our family chose to homeschool. Homeschooling is not for everyone, but it works well for many families. Being able to engage with your children and the world day in and day out is a mind-expanding, growth-enhancing family experience. It can also be tiring and frustrating, just like many other aspects of parenting, but the positive far outweighs the negative.

Again, you may have to be creative about balancing work time with home time if both parents are working (or if you are a single parent). But it can be done if you're interested. Not all homeschooling families are made up of the stay-at-home mom and support-the-family dad. Often both parents each work part time, or the stay-at-home parent has a small home business to bring in extra income. Once the children get big enough to play and learn without constant supervision, the whole process gets even easier.

Homeschooling itself does not have to be expensive, although, as with many things, some homeschooling families go that route by purchasing costly curricula, teachers' services, supplies, etc. You don't have to do that: everything you need can be found at your library and in your community. Another money-saving benefit is that your kids won't have all that peer pressure that makes them want to buy the latest in designer clothes and electronic gadgetry. They'll be happy dressed in secondhand clothes and playing with yard-sale toys.

Over one million children are now homeschooled in the United States. It's not hard to find resources, support, and other families to spend time with. For more information, check the Internet, your library, or your newspaper's calendar of events.

Keep an open mind. Look into working part time. Watch your expenses. Think about your children's future. You will do them — and yourself — a big favor if you take the time to develop a close and lasting relationship with them. That's hard to do if you only see each other for an hour or two every weekday.

Redefine a "good education"

Every parent wants the best for their child and for themselves. Many people think this means getting a "good education," but what does that mean, exactly? Private school during the elementary and high school years? Four years at an Ivy League college? Graduate and post-graduate degrees?

Think about your own education, where you received it, how long it lasted, and what it cost. Did those years and that money get you what you wanted? Are you pleased with your education? Did it prepare you for who and where you are today? Did it acknowledge your particular gifts and skills, challenge you, and get you ready for the "real world"?

A college education is not for everyone. Trade school or apprenticeship may work better for some. Several years of travel, VISTA/Americorps, or the Peace Corps may educate in ways that even the best school cannot. Some people learn better by doing hands-on work; others relish the printed page and the exchange of ideas that comes from classroom learning. What kind of learner are you? What kind of learners are your children? What kind of work do you — and they — like and have the energy, innate skills, and constitution for?

Many people dream of being an actor, popular singer, or athlete, but not everyone has the inborn gifts for that. Others want to pursue a scientific field and have a mind to match. Still others don't want to punch a time clock and would enjoy the challenge of working for themselves. Then there are those whose true gift is working with people, and no one had to teach them how.

Before you, or your children, become saddled with educational debt, think first about what you really want to learn and what you want to do with your lives. If you're unsure, there are plenty of career-choice quizzes on the Internet and in books at your library. Take some time to think this through, because if college is the ultimate choice, it will be one of the biggest investments you ever make. There may be another way to get what you want. If you do choose college, find one whose price is within your means.

The argument that no one can get a good job or succeed in life without a college education is simply not true. I know many people who have been successful — personally, professionally, and financially — without a college degree, and I'll bet you do, too.

Expose them to other cultures

Our world is big and beautiful. We are a tapestry of colors, foods, languages, houses, and ways of life. One way to appreciate your life more and learn how it could be different is to learn about other cultures, continents, countries, peoples, and ways of life.

Travel is one way to do this, and it doesn't have to be expensive, as has been covered in Chapter Twelve: Travel. Families can find inexpensive ways to see the world together by biking or hiking, camping or staying in hostels, preparing much of their own food, and skipping the tourist traps. It is possible to do a house exchange with a family from another part of the world or another part of the country. There are international volunteer work programs where you can work as part of a multigenerational and multicultural team clearing trails, repairing buildings, and starting gardens.

You can also find different cultures closer to home. If you live in a city, it is easy enough to go to Chinatown, Little Italy, or any of the other areas that are not part of your ethnic habitat. There is always music and food to be enjoyed, often for little cost or simply by strolling the streets. If you live in a more homogenous region, you may be able to travel just a little further afield to discover another culture. In the Northeast, for example, the Quebecois influence is strong in certain areas, just as the Mexican and Native American influence is easily felt in the Southwest.

Those of us who remember *National Geographic* films from our days in school know that other cultures can be easily experienced through books, magazines, and videos. Your library will have all you need to take a trip around the world from the comfort of your own home. Hang maps in your house, and photo collages of people from around the world. Locate current events on your world map, and talk with your kids about how the events relate to the people who live there.

It's important to remember that people from cultures other than our own are not on display, but rather that we are humans together on this small planet who have our own foods, living situations, clothing, music, religions, and ways of being, none of which are necessarily better or worse than any other, just different. Raising our children to understand and respect diversity is a great gift to them and to the planet. Once they learn that most children in the world go without computers, televisions, and cars, they can begin to understand that frugality is not weird, but the norm.

Teach and learn conflict resolution skills

Just as we have different cultures and ways of doing things, we also have conflicts, large and small, wherever we go. Sometimes these conflicts are solved by peaceable means, sometimes they're not. In an age-appropriate way, teach your children how to solve conflicts without hitting, biting, saying mean things, or destroying someone else's property. If you're unsure how to go about this, check your library for books on conflict resolution with kids: there are many.

The place to start is with talking and understanding that what someone actually says may not be the whole picture. There is a wonderful story about two children fighting over the last orange and getting into a big screaming match about it. Turns out, with some verbal prompting by a third person, that one child wanted the peel for a recipe, and the other wanted the juice. By talking about it and expressing what they really wanted with the help of a neutral person, they were both able to get exactly that. (No one has to run out and buy more oranges, either!)

Consider taking that neutral role when helping your children solve a problem. Have them talk about it; don't just order one to give the toy to the other. They may be able to come up with their own solution to the problem; all the better, because they will probably be more apt to follow their own plan than your orders. Teach them to do this with each other and with their friends. It may take some time at first, but in the long run they'll develop important skills that will last them a lifetime. Understanding how to handle conflict peaceably is just one step in the process of developing the personal awareness and respectfulness that is the foundation of frugality.

Have them help you with what you're doing

Our children learn about the world by watching and imitating those around them. They want to do what you do, whatever that is. Choose wisely, and ask them to help. I have never met a small child that didn't want to hold the dustpan, or try to use the broom. Depending on their age, they love to help with cooking, folding laundry, repairing clothes, harvesting vegetables, changing the oil, feeding the animals, counting money, or doing the dishes. If you practice a craft such as knitting or woodworking, have them help you as appropriate. Don't worry that the task may take longer or be messier: that's how they learn.

If you do any kind of paid work from home, see if there's a way they can participate. They may be able to stuff envelopes or boxes, stick on mailing labels, create computer graphics, lay out your business documents, do the bookkeeping, or answer the phone. Depending on your business and the age and skill of the child, they may be able to contribute in meaningful ways. If you don't work at home at all, bring them to work with you, if possible, several times a year.

All of this helps them understand about life and the realities of keeping a household together and doing real work in the world. They will understand more about what's in that briefcase, or why you're so tired at the end of the day. They will feel competent when they master a skill. They may find something that enchants them enough that they take it up as a life path of their own. It's also a great time to talk and be together — a sure way to develop a close and lasting relationship. As a side effect, they will learn many skills that will help them come to frugality naturally as adults.

Teach them about money

Money is a sensitive subject with many people. But, like sex, it's just a fact of life. Once you become more comfortable with money yourself, you will feel comfortable talking about it with your kids. (You should try the same thing with sex!)

Children love to go to the store. Teach them about the prices of things and the importance of comparison shopping. Show them the different coins and bills and have them count the change. Have them help you with monthly bill paying and your monthly income and expenses tabulation. Make money a regular part of conversation.

Show them your bank statement, your credit-card bill, the title to your car, your income-tax statement, and the deed to your house. Play Monopoly with them. If you choose to give them an allowance, talk about the importance of saving a portion, donating a portion to charity, and keeping track of their income and expenses. Teach them how to balance a checkbook. Include them in the decision-making when you're considering buying or selling something. Tell them how much money you save, about compound interest, and about the stock market.

As our society descends deeper and deeper into debt, teaching your children about money is one of the best things you can do to help them have a solid and sustainable future. If money is real to them, they will not have to be convinced of the value of being frugal as a way to have the freedom to do the things they want to do as adults.

Encourage them to listen to their bodies

Our bodies do many things and tell us many things, if we would only listen. We know when we are tired, when we are sick, when we've played a sport too long, or when we have ridden our bike too far.

We also know when we're hungry, but our society is set up on a three-meal-a-day system at pretty specific times, and that's when we're supposed to eat. Not everyone gets hungry at those times, or that often. If we learn to listen to our bodies and our true physical hunger (versus emotional "mouth" hunger), we will eat what our bodies actually need, when they need it. It's a frugal — aware and respectful — way to eat.

Feeding schedules for infants go in and out of vogue. Try letting your baby or toddler ask for food (in their own way) before you direct them to it. Try letting them choose what they want to eat before you put it in front of them.

If you haven't done this before, you may need to prompt them with age-appropriate choices (Peas or carrots? Rice or noodles? An apple or blueberries?). If they ask for food not too long after they've eaten, ask them if they're really hungry, and explain what this means if they don't understand.

This is not easy. Many parents fear that their children will eat nothing but sweets and starches if given free rein. But the human body is a miraculous thing: it generally knows what it wants, and the child just has to be taught to listen. It is important to do this with guidance, but after a starch-heavy day, you'll probably find that your child will want fruits or vegetables. Nutritionists say that it's not necessarily important to eat balanced meals, and that a child (or an adult) will automatically balance their diet over several days to a week, given the option.

This may mean that for a while, or for some meals, the whole family does not eat together. Try not to be worried about that, and find another way to be together. This is a good time for something fun like a board game, playing music, or going for a walk.

Remember that children learn by watching you, so try to eat when you're hungry — and eat what you're truly craving — as well.

Listening to our bodies also goes for sleep, exercise, and taking care of ourselves when we don't feel well. Just as we encourage our toddlers to nap, sometimes big people need naps, too. Try not to have a rigid bedtime schedule: different bodies at different ages have different needs for food and rest. Make exercise time a family time when you all go for a walk or a bike ride or just toss a Frisbee around in the yard. Learn what your body needs, and help them learn what their body needs.

Encourage inner direction versus outer direction

School and the working world are set up to direct us to do certain things at certain times. Except in a handful of professions and in a few schools, creativity and inner direction are not encouraged. But we're all born with it: we cry for warm milk or a diaper change when we need it (unless we're started out on a rigid schedule). We know when to sleep and when to be active. We understand when we need some exercise or when to stop playing computer games if we only listen to our bodies and our minds.

Encourage this innate skill in your children (and yourself) by respecting what they already know about themselves. Some kids need to watch for a while before they jump into an activity. Some kids need noise or movement to be able to focus. Some kids need absolute quiet and a tidy space. Some kids can do the same activity for hours; others need to work for short spans of time. Watch your children to learn their ways.

Just as with learning to eat when we're hungry and to sleep when we're tired, we can all develop our inner direction. Having a strong sense of inner direction can help everyone throughout life as we make choices about work, home, marriage, leisure activities, and the way we spend money. Having a strong sense of inner direction can help us say no to unhealthy or destructive behaviors, boring activities, a crumbling relationship, or a job that's not a good fit. We all need this skill, since the "outer" voices are so strong, and it's best to start as young as possible. The way to reach that self-awareness is to learn to listen to our inner direction and have our actions fit in with our values and who we are inside.

Be yourself and be honest

Being frugal is not just about money. It's about being who we are as individuals, and making conscious choices about how we spend our money and our time. It's about understanding the difference between our wants and our needs, and how our emotional lives affect all of it. We're not perfect, and we shouldn't pretend to be.

Our children are not fools. They can see through a lie in an instant. They know when the people around them are sad or happy or angry. They can also see through a parent who speaks a "do as I say, not as I do" line.

Talk about how you're feeling, and encourage your kids to do the same. It's OK to say that you had a bad day at work or that you're sad because your best friend is very sick. It's OK to say that you don't want to play right now because you need a little time to be by yourself or because you have to make an important phone call. It's OK to be silly, blow bubbles, play croquet, or roll down a hill.

Just because we're parents doesn't mean we can't be ourselves. We have our own collection of hopes and dreams, fears and sorrows. We do have to be careful not to push our dreams and fears onto our children, and it's not appropriate to discuss our marital problems with them, either. It is all right to tell them the story of when we got scared of a spider the first time we went camping, or that we're thinking about changing jobs. They're learning from us with everything that we say or don't say, do or don't do. They're watching for cues to learn how to be in the world. It's our job to teach them the fullness of life and also to live our own lives fully at the same time.

A final word about children

Having children is a great adventure and a wonderful blessing, but there are already too many people on our planet. If you don't think you want children, don't be pressured by friends, family, or society to have them. If you have not yet had children and want them, consider having only one biological child. If you want a larger family (or are unable to have biological children), consider adoption or foster care. If you have more than one biological child, it is even more important that you raise them to respect their stuff and their money and to remember that their actions affect not only themselves but also their family, their friends, and eventually many other people on the planet. As people living in the most affluent society on the earth, it is our responsibility to reduce unnecessary consumption and learn to share. This is the essence of frugality and is vital to everyone's survival and everyone's ability to have a comfortable and meaningful life.

Resources

In addition to the books, organizations, and websites mentioned throughout the text, below are some additional resources for you on your path to freedom through frugality. A word to the wise: there are many, many websites with "penny pinching" tips and downloadable coupons, but most of them simply tell you how to buy stuff for less money. That's fine advice if you really need something. I find, however, that many of them just encourage you to spend more money on stuff you don't really need. Remember, in the long run, the best way to save money is to not spend it at all!

For information about air drying your clothes, drying supplies, and the latest on the legal battles in different states: **www.laundrylist.org**

For nonelectric household appliances and tools: **www.lehmans.com**

For information and support for families trying to live more sustainably, contact the Center for a New American Dream: **www.newdream.org**

For information about the ecological footprint and living on less: **www.myfootprint.org**

For general resources and support for sustainable and simple living: **www.simpleliving.net**

For online support using the *Your Money or Your Life* program: **www.financialintegrity.org**

For frugal travel tips: **frugaltraveler.blogs.nytimes.com**

About the author

To keep life interesting, Jane Dwinell has done many things over the years, both paid and volunteer. She has been (and, in some cases, continues to be) a nurse, farmer, business owner, chef, carpenter, salsa maker, maple-syrup producer, guardian ad litem, teacher, hospice chaplain, parish minister, author, consultant, quilt maker, knitter, actress, singer, yoga practitioner, long-distance runner, downhill skier, disc-golf player, live-aboard boater, mother, daughter, partner, sister, aunt, and friend.

Jane and her partner, Sky Yardley, currently divide their time between New Orleans, Vermont, and France. She is available for speaking engagements: contact her via www.spiritoflifepublishing.com.